Plumbing Do-It-Yourself For Dummies®

Your Tools Shopping List

No matter what job you're doing, you'll always be more effective if you have the right tools. Here's a shopping list of many of the plumbing tools you'll need to do the projects in this book. And check out Chapter 4 for pictures and descriptions.

- Adjustable wrench
- Locking adjustable wrench
- Groove-joint pliers
- Pipe wrench
- Flanged plunger
- Hand-crank auger
- Toilet auger
- Plastic blade putty knife
- Screwdrivers
- Wire brush
- Strainer wrench
- Lock-nut or spud wrench
- Tubing cutter
- Flux brush
- Propane torch
- Spark igniter
- Fiber or safety shield
- Caulk gun
- Files
- Tape measure
- Utility knife
- Hacksaw
- Tubing benders
- Hammer

Safety Equipment

These items are necessary for any do-it-yourselfer, not just ones with a predisposition for plumbing:

- Safety goggles
- Hearing protection
- Leather gloves
- Heavy-duty rubber gloves
- GFCI-protected extension cords
- Fire extinguisher

Know When It's Time to Hire a Pro

When the following situations arise, it's best to call a professional. So get to know a good plumber in your area, and keep his or her name and number handy for emergencies.

- **Low water pressure throughout the house:** Several factors can cause this problem: obstructions (rust or debris) in the water lines, which can start at the meter and run all the way to the faucet *aerators* (small strainers on the end of the spigot); low water pressure from the city supply or a well; or even poor supply-line design. A good plumber knows how to analyze the problem.

- **No hot water:** It's obvious *what* happened, but unless the hot water tank is leaking, it may take a while to find out *why*. If the tank is electric, it could be a bad heating element, a tripped circuit breaker or blown fuse, a faulty thermostat, or a bad overload switch. On gas heaters, thermocouple burners and igniters can fail. If the heater needs to be replaced, think twice before attempting to do it yourself. Remember, your plumber can carry the new one to the basement, hook it up, make sure that it works properly, and dispose of the old one.

- **Sewer line stoppage:** If you've tried all the tricks you know to get your sewer line to drain properly, yet backups continue, you probably have a bad plug in the line that runs out to the main sewer. (Tree roots are often the cause.) Rather than rent one of the big sewer rodding machines that you may break — or that may damage your sewer — call a plumber or drain-cleaning service. If they get in trouble, they'll make the repairs.

- **Frozen pipes:** If a pipe freezes, close the main water shutoff valve before attempting to thaw the pipe and open a faucet nearby. Check carefully to see whether the pipe has already burst or cracked. If it's bad news, you may need a plumber. If not, hair dryers and heat guns are the safest ways to thaw a pipe. If you must use a propane torch, do so with great care — old, dry wood (which usually surrounds pipes) catches fire easily. Even if the pipe isn't burst or cracked, you still may want to call a plumber: Some plumbers simply replace a section of frozen pipe rather than thaw it.

- **Extensive water line damage (usually caused by freezing):** Repairing the problem can take up much of your valuable time. It's better to pay a plumber so that you can earn money at your regular job.

DO-IT-YOURSELF

Plumbing

FOR

DUMMIES®

DO-IT-YOURSELF

Plumbing

FOR

DUMMIES®

by Donald R. Prestly

BICENTENNIAL
1807
WILEY
2007
BICENTENNIAL

Wiley Publishing, Inc.

Plumbing Do-It-Yourself For Dummies®

Published by
Wiley Publishing, Inc.
111 River St.
Hoboken, NJ 07030-5774

WILEY

About the Author

Donald R. Prestly is a former Senior Editor for *HANDY Magazine* for The Handyman Club of America as well as a former Associate Editor for *The Family Handyman Magazine.* In addition to nearly 20 years of writing and doing home improvement projects, he spent several years as a manager for one of the Midwest's largest home centers. Throw in the everyday upkeep requirements of being a homeowner, dealing with the same problems and repairs as other homeowners, and it's clear that he has the background and expertise to help do-it-yourselfers tackle home plumbing repairs. *Plumbing Do-It-Yourself For Dummies* is Don's second *For Dummies* book; he's also the author of *Kitchen Remodeling For Dummies,* published in 2003.

Dedication

I dedicate this book to the thousands of homeowners who have heard cries of "Fix that leaky faucet!" or "The toilet's clogged!" It's important for you to know that you're not alone in your plumbing problems and fixes. The plumbing department in almost every hardware store and home center is one of the busiest departments in the store (if not *the* busiest). And it's usually filled with anxious and sometimes frantic homeowners who need the right stuff, right now, to save the house and sometimes even their relationships! For all of you who want to tackle plumbing or at least understand it better, this book is for you.

Author's Acknowledgments

So where do I begin? Over 20 years ago, I left the world of home improvement sales and management and got started in the industry known as DIY. Little did I know or could have envisioned that I'd end up writing my second home improvement book for the great team at Wiley Publishing. All their books make information interesting, understandable, and, most importantly, fun! A big thanks to Tom Reed at Kreber Photography for the great how-to photos and a huge thank you to Senior Project Editor (and my day-to-day working editor) Tim Gallan.

Publisher's Acknowledgments

We're proud of this book; please send us your comments through our Dummies online registration form located at www.dummies.com/register/.

Some of the people who helped bring this book to market include the following:

Acquisitions, Editorial, and Media Development

Senior Project Editor: Tim Gallan

Acquisitions Editor: Tracy Boggier

Senior Copy Editor: Elizabeth Rea

Editorial Program Coordinator: Erin Calligan Mooney

Editorial Managers: Christine Meloy Beck, Michelle Hacker

Editorial Assistants: Joe Niesen, David Lutton, Leeann Harney

Photographer: Tom Reed, Kreber Photography

Cartoons: Rich Tennant (www.the5thwave.com)

Composition Services

Project Coordinator: Kristie Rees

Layout and Graphics: Shawn Frazier, Shelley Norris, Kathie Rickard, Brent Savage

Anniversary Logo Design: Richard Pacifico

Proofreaders: Laura Albert, Jessica Kramer, Shannon Ramsey

Indexer: Potomac Indexing, LLC

Publishing and Editorial for Consumer Dummies

Diane Graves Steele, Vice President and Publisher, Consumer Dummies

Joyce Pepple, Acquisitions Director, Consumer Dummies

Kristin A. Cocks, Product Development Director, Consumer Dummies

Michael Spring, Vice President and Publisher, Travel

Kelly Regan, Editorial Director, Travel

Publishing for Technology Dummies

Andy Cummings, Vice President and Publisher, Dummies Technology/General User

Composition Services

Gerry Fahey, Vice President of Production Services

Debbie Stailey, Director of Composition Services

Contents at a Glance

Table of Contents

Introduction

Plumbing *Do-It-Yourself For Dummies* shows you how to deal with most runs, leaks, and drips of your home's plumbing system and gives you confidence to tackle some seemingly professional-level repairs. I provide information here on kitchen fixtures (both the faucet and the sink) and bathroom fixtures (toilets, tubs, and showers). I also show you how a residential plumbing system is designed as well as how it operates and what's needed to make it work right.

I hope you find this book not only packed full of information but also fun to use. My years of working with customers every day in one of the country's major home centers, along with my decade and a half of researching and writing about — and doing! — home repairs gives me real-life insight into what you can expect to find when it comes to fixing your home's plumbing problems. And, believe me, you will eventually encounter problems.

About This Book

This book is intended to provide step-by-step instructions on repairing the most common types of plumbing fixtures. I'd need much more space to cover every brand or style of plumbing fixture in homes or being sold today. But the information I provide will equip you to make repairs or, at the very least, give you the knowledge to explain the problem to a plumbing professional (also known as "the plumber") and understand what the plumber is doing if you need to hire a professional to make the repair.

The information in the book is organized into five parts, and the chapters within each part cover repairs to specific types of fixtures. You can read every chapter or pick and choose the ones that are of interest to you. Either way, you come away with the tips and techniques to keep your home's plumbing system working right!

For many of the repairs, you'll be dealing with nuisance issues — for example, a kitchen faucet that drips or a toilet that occasionally "runs" for a short time. Some of the repairs, however, require immediate attention to prevent damage to your home. A perfect example is when there's water leaking out from under your toilet bowl! Fix it ASAP or you could be spending hundreds (maybe thousands?) of dollars to repair structural damage due to rot.

And if you're not sure what you need to do first, seek out the advice of the folks at your local hardware store or home center. They can help guide you through a plumbing repair that you're not familiar with or comfortable tackling, often with success!

Conventions Used in This Book

Most projects in this book intentionally have more photos than text. Seeing how a repair is done is just as critical as reading how to do it.

All Web addresses appear in `monofont`.

Foolish Assumptions

Plumbing repairs can seem too hard for many do-it-yourselfers. In reality, you, the homeowner, can handle many plumbing problems as long as you're armed with the proper information. In writing this book, I made the following assumptions about you:

- You're interested in understanding plumbing repairs, not only to gain the confidence and know-how to take them on but also to save money by making repairs yourself.
- You probably aren't familiar with plumbing repairs and may never have attempted making any before. But you want to try!
- You want to know more about how a repair should be done so that if you have to hire someone to do it, you can be confident that you're getting a good deal on quality work.

How This Book Is Organized

This book is divided into five parts. Part I introduces you to the world of plumbing. Parts II, III, and IV explain how to make repairs to the most common plumbing problems, whether in the kitchen or bathroom. Part V presents the usual top-ten lists found in all *For Dummies* books.

Part I: Getting to Know Your Plumbing System

This part explains the various components that make up a residential plumbing system and describes how the system works. It discusses the how's and why's of getting a permit for some projects and where to turn for guidance when you feel stuck. It also goes into detail with regard to plumbing tools.

Part II: Faucets and Sinks

This part shows how to repair the most commonly found types of kitchen and bathroom faucets in homes. It also shows how to keep your sink leak-free and in best-use condition, covering things from caulking the seam between the sink and countertop to replacing a sink drain basket assembly and drain lines.

Part III: Tubs and Showers

This part shows how to keep your tub faucet and showerhead working their best. No leaks, no drips, and the best water-flow possible. It walks you through the steps of sealing joints between the plumbing fixtures and the walls, preventing costly repairs. It also shows you how to deal with clogged or slow-running drains.

Part IV: Toilets

This part deals with the most important plumbing fixture in the house! It shows you how to make a toilet run efficiently and eliminate the "phantom flush" (seeping water) by replacing any or all old or defective parts in the tank. It also illustrates how to deal with a leak under the bowl and prevent damage to the bathroom floor and subfloor. Finally, this part shows you the best ways to deal with and remove or clear the dreaded clogged toilet!

Part V: The Part of Tens

No *For Dummies* book would be complete without the Part of Tens. In this part, you uncover ways to deal with noisy and frozen pipes, what to do before you call a plumbing professional, and what you must do to keep yourself safe when making plumbing repairs.

Icons Used in This Book

This book is loaded with the following helpful icons that point out key information:

Make a note when you see this icon. It points out time-saving, money-saving, and keep-you-from-pulling-out-your-hair advice.

Think of this icon as the flashing light and red flag alerting you to things that have the potential to cause you and your plumbing helpers physical harm or make your repair more difficult.

Where to Go from Here

I recommend that you start with Part I, especially if you're completely or even fairly unfamiliar with plumbing in general. If you feel comfortable and confident that you can make some plumbing repairs, then feel free to find the repair for your specific plumbing problem and have at it!

Remember, it really doesn't matter where you start just as long as you address plumbing issues in your home that need attention and fixing. I'm confident that after you attempt (and successfully complete!) your first do-it-yourself plumbing project, you'll be ready to tackle virtually any others that come along in the years to come.

Part I
Getting to Know Your Plumbing System

In this part . . .

There's plenty at work when you turn on a faucet or flush a toilet in your house. And if you want to tackle home plumbing problems, you need to know what you're dealing with. The chapters in this part cover a wide range of plumbing basics, from knowing your limits to understanding residential plumbing systems, from recognizing different kinds of pipes and fittings to being informed about plumbing codes and requirements. To cap it all off, I share recommendations on stocking your plumbing toolbox so that you're well-equipped to handle plumbing problems around your house.

Chapter 1

Understanding Plumbing

To many people, a home's plumbing system is perceived as being extremely complex with lots of parts that only a professional plumber is qualified to work on. In some cases, it's true that you're better off in terms of both time and money calling in a professional; for example, only the most advanced do-it-yourselfer should consider taking on replacing the main drainpipe for a home's toilets. But for many plumbing jobs around the average home, even a plumbing novice can make the repairs the right way with good information to follow. And that's what this book is all about — providing the most up-to-date plumbing project information so that even a beginner can tackle many of the most common residential plumbing problems.

Establishing Your Plumbing Limits

If you consider yourself moderately handy (and be honest with yourself when you assess your plumbing skills), then you should be able to tackle most of the projects in this book. Remember, however, that plumbing repairs can be time-consuming and therefore require one important trait — patience! I've tackled (and successfully completed, I might add!) more plumbing repairs than I care to count. But I'm the first to admit that many of my projects took twice as long to complete as I had planned for. Some of that extra time was the result of buyer-error, less-than-cooperative existing plumbing, and not allowing for extra visits to the hardware store or home center. My plumbing projects have taught me that even a well-planned project can run into unexpected problems and delays. And when that happens, you should be ready and willing to call out for an extra helping of patience.

Ensuring Successful Plumbing Adventures

Working in a logical step-by-step order makes repairs — plumbing and otherwise — go more smoothly and keeps you safe. Trying to speed up a step or cut a corner only leads to an inferior and potentially dangerous repair. For example, virtually every plumbing repair project starts with turning off the water. I instruct you to do it upfront in most of the projects in this book, and it seems like a fairly obvious first step. But don't be surprised if you get soaked or sprayed when you disconnect that faucet or toilet valve because you forgot Step 1!

Making plumbing repairs isn't and shouldn't be frightening or utterly impossible. Today's plumbing product manufacturers have made installation instructions pretty easy to understand, and many companies have toll-free numbers or online technical support departments to turn to with questions. Plus, most home centers and hardware stores have at least a few salespeople who really do know their stuff! But it's important to remember that if you feel uncomfortable attempting a specific repair, don't be ashamed to call in a plumber.

Before you start a plumbing project, assess and evaluate if the project is something you can or even want to attempt. If you answer "no" or even "maybe," consider hiring a plumber from the start instead of starting the project yourself. You'll save money by only paying the plumber for the work and not for having to fix or undo the work you attempted. Here are a few plumbing realities to keep in mind when considering a project:

✔ Plumbing repairs require you to get your hands dirty. Some can get really messy — that's just the way it is.

✔ Some plumbing repairs require some physical labor and may require helpers. For example, lifting a toilet can be a job for two people, so don't be afraid to ask someone to help.

✔ You may have to work in some pretty uncomfortable and cramped areas, like under the kitchen sink or overhead when soldering copper supply lines.

The Residential Plumbing System

For the most part, the majority of your home's plumbing system is hidden in walls, floors, and ceilings. The parts you see — the fixtures and faucets — are only the end of the line. The lines and pipes that get water to you and waste away from you are the guts of the system. However, understanding a home plumbing system is really quite simple.

Most residential plumbing systems have three components:

✔ A water supply system that includes getting both hot and cold water to fixtures

✔ The fixtures that deliver the water

✔ A drain/waste/vent, or DWV, system

Figure 1-1 shows clearly how each of these components fit together to form the plumbing system.

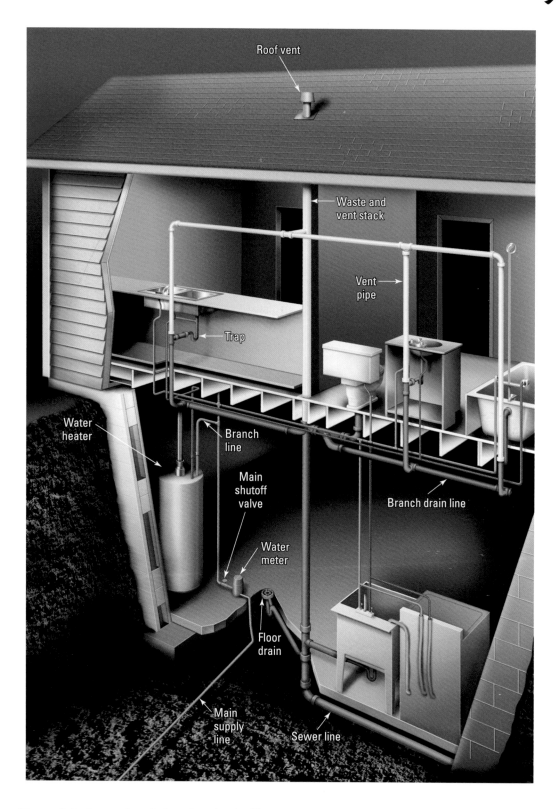

Figure 1-1: An overview of a home's entire plumbing system.

The supply side: Water comes in

The supply system, which is highlighted in Figure 1-2, begins where the water enters the house through a main supply line or water main. The water source is either provided by a municipal water company or a private underground well located on the property. If the source is a municipal supplier, the water runs through a water meter so that water useage can be recorded and the homeowner billed accordingly. There's no meter on a private well.

Homes built before 1960 generally have galvanized pipe for the original supply lines, whereas homes built after 1960 usually have rigid copper pipe supply lines. Some of today's new homes have plastic supply line pipes; this setup now is being accepted by most local plumbing codes. I cover supply line pipes in more detail in Chapter 3.

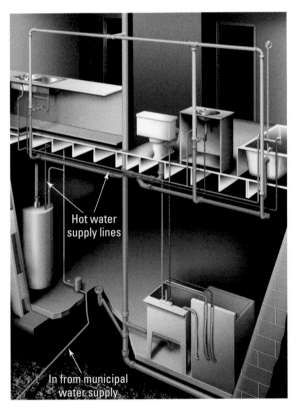

Figure 1-2: The water supply system.

Is your water safe?

Municipal water companies regularly test the water they supply to homes to make sure that it's safe to drink. If you have a private well, it's your responsibility to test the water for purity. Most areas require private wells to be tested at least once a year. Check with your city's water officials for the testing frequency requirements in your area. They can also provide you with a list of companies that do qualified well water testing.

Even if your water is safe to drink, it could still have tastes and odors that you find less than desirable. Water filters, both whole-house and point-of-use, can eliminate or greatly reduce poor tasting or smelling water. Check out your local home center or hardware store for the type of filters or filtering sytems that are recommended for your area.

Within just feet of where the main line enters the home, a branch line splits off the main and connects to your water heater. From the water heater, the hot water line runs parallel to the cold water line to fixtures (including sinks, bathtubs, showers, and laundry tubs) and appliances (including washing machines, dishwashers, and water softeners). Toilets and exterior faucets (called *sillcocks*) are fixtures that require only cold water. A refrigerator icemaker also only requires cold water, which often is tapped off of a nearby cold water line.

The water pressure to the fixtures in your home is determined by the size of the pipe's inside diameter. The larger the pipe, the greater the pressure, so if your water pressure is too weak, the problem may be undersized pipes. The pipe entering the house usually has an inside diameter of 1 or 1¼ inches. Soon after the main line enters the house, the pipe reduces to ¾ inch. Pipes that carry water to rooms throughout the house have an inside diameter of either ¾ or ½ inch. Pipes that supply water to each fixture are usually ½-inch inside diameter to the shutoff valve and then ¼-inch inside diameter to the fixture.

Drain, waste, and vent: Water goes out

Getting rid of used or waste water is achieved through your home's DWV system, which stands for drain, waste, and vent. The drains (D) are the pieces that hold and then carry the waste water to the main drain lines (W). Without a constant air supply, a vacuum would build up in the drain lines, eventually stopping the water from flowing; To prevent this, each DWV system requires adequate and proper venting (V). The drain pipes use gravity to carry waste and waste water away from fixtures, drains, and appliances. The waste water is carried out of the house through the main drain line to a municipal sewer system or a septic tank (if you have a private well). Figure 1-3 shows the system in detail.

Never install or alter your home's DWV system without consulting a building inspector. All three parts of this system must be installed according to precise specifications in order to work properly and safely.

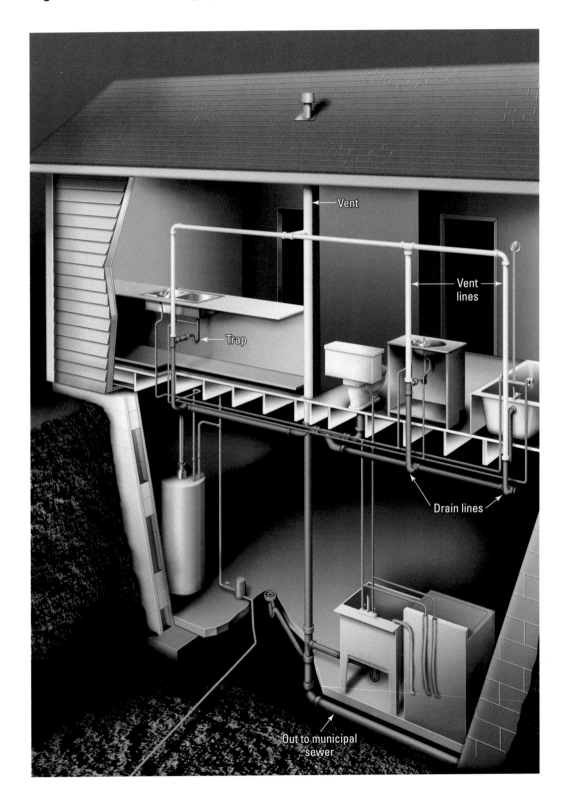

Figure 1-3: The DWV system.

The main stack

The primary component in a DWV system is the *main stack* (sometimes called the *main soil stack*). The stack pipe is usually 3 or 4 inches in diameter and made of plastic or cast iron. Located near the center of the house, the main stack goes down below the basement floor or under the house slab (if there's no basement) and empties into the sewer or septic tank. The main stack also has a vent pipe connected to it that extends up through the roof. Without the vent, the waste water wouldn't flow quickly enough to clear the pipes, eventually leading to severe main line clogs. A house may also have one or two secondary vent stacks located above and off the bathroom drain lines.

Branch drain lines carry water from specific fixtures to the main stack. The branch lines are smaller diameter than the main stack — usually 1½ or 2 inches in diameter. Drain lines must be sloped so that water runs freely to the main stack. The slope is usually ¼ inch per foot. For branch lines, local plumbing codes require special fittings that have sweeping turns and not abrupt angles that could lead to clogged pipes.

Traps

Traps are a critical part of the DWV system. These curved pieces of pipe hold water inside the curve that prevents sewer gas from backing up into the house. Each time the drain in a fixture or appliance is used, the standing water is flushed down the drain and replaced with new water.

Vents

Venting is required for the DWV system to operate properly. Without an air passageway behind the water flow, the system would run slow and gurgle. Each fixture is required to be vented, but you don't need a vent stack through the roof for each fixture. If you did, your home's roof would look like a smokestack-filled industrial factory! Individual fixture vent stacks often are connected to a revent pipe that eventually connects to the main stack vent in the roof.

If one or more of your fixtures runs slow, or if a toilet gurgles when you flush it and you know it's not clogged, chances are good that the vent stack is blocked. This fix is best left to a professional plumber to determine if it's just a blocked vent or if the plumbing itself is improperly installed and needs correction.

Septic systems: Don't mess with them!

If your home is outside city or suburb limits, it probably isn't connected to a municipal water system, which means that you have your own well and septic system.

Your home's water supply and DWV systems are usually the same as those in a house that's connected to a municipal water system and sewer (see the earlier sections "The supply side: Water comes in" and "Drain, waste, and vent: Water goes out.") The difference is that in a typical septic system, the waste water flows from the house out through a main stack into the septic tank, as shown in Figure 1-4. The tank usually is made of concrete or plastic.

A septic system has two tanks: the primary tank that collects most solids and the secondary tank that collects the remaining solids. The solids or sludge sink to the bottom of the primary tank while baffles inside the tank trap the scum (floating grease and soap) so that only liquid (called *effluent liquid*) leaves the tank. The effluent liquid moves by gravity through a drain pipe and empties into the septic system's leach field, where the effluent liquid is broken down by naturally occurring microbes. Then it either evaporates or is absorbed by the soil and plants.

A septic system needs to be monitored and either cleaned or pumped on a regular basis, although not every year because each time waste water flows into the tanks, an equal amount of effluent liquid is pushed out the other end into the leach field. If the system is properly sized for your house and properly installed, it probably only needs to be pumped every three to four years. Use a wooden pole to check the sludge level in the tanks once a year. If the tank is almost half filled, hire someone to pump the system. If the leach field starts to smell bad, or if water backs up out of the drains, call a septic company immediately! The cause may just be a clog that's easily cleared if you catch it soon enough. Leave the work of repairing a septic system to professionals.

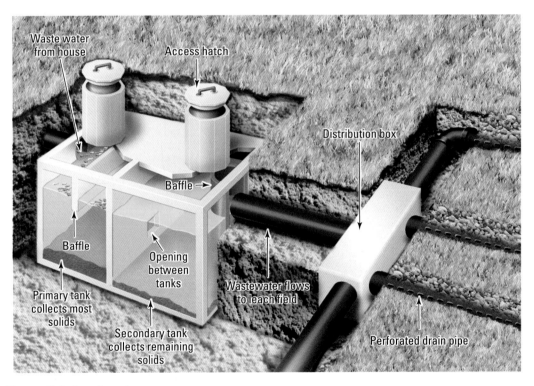

Figure 1-4: A septic system.

Chapter 2

Fetch Me My Pipe and Fittings!

Without the two basic components of a plumbing system — water supply pipes and fittings — water could never reach you in an efficient manner. The pipes and fittings you use for the repairs shown in this book probably will be copper, PVC, or ABS (see the next section for coverage of these pipe types). However, you may encounter other types while working with an existing plumbing system. For example, homes built before 1960 have galvanized steel pipe for water supply lines and usually cast iron DWV pipe systems (for an explanation of DWV systems, turn to Chapter 1).

Because this book is really intended for beginning do-it-yourself plumbers, I recommend that you call in a professional plumber if your home is older and has galvanized steel or cast iron pipe.

Pipes

Here's a quick look at types of pipes commonly used in homes, beginning with the pipes used for DWV systems.

✔ **Cast iron:** Most homes built before 1960 have cast iron pipes (see Figure 2-1) used for the vertical drain and vent stacks. Cast iron also may have been used for the horizontal drain lines. Cast iron is very durable and lasts for decades, but it can rust over time. It's not uncommon for a section of pipe, a fitting, or a coupling to rust through while the rest of the cast iron system remains fine. A professional plumber can replace rusted sections and connecting pieces with plastic (PVC or ABS) paired with the correct transition fittings.

✔ **Plastic:** Plastic pipe comes in two primary varieties: ABS (acrylonitrile-buta-diene-styrene) and PVC (polyvinyl-chloride). In general, plastic has been the pipe material of choice since the mid-1970s because it's inexpensive and easy to use. You simply glue the joints together using a primer and a liquid cement made for the particular type of pipe you're installing, whether ABS or PVC.

   • **ABS:** This black pipe (see Figure 2-1) was the first plastic pipe to be used in residential plumbing systems. Now, some regions and cities don't allow ABS in new construction because some joints have been known to come loose. Check with your local plumbing inspector if you want to use ABS pipe.

- **PVC:** This white or cream colored pipe (see Figure 2-1) is the most commonly used pipe for drain lines. It's strong, virtually untouchable by chemicals, and seems to last forever! The engineering rating and diameter is stamped on the outside of the pipe; Schedule 40 PVC is the most common and is accepted as strong enough for residential drain lines in most locales. Check with your plumbing inspector to be certain. Schedule 80 PVC is sometimes used for cold-water supply lines; however, many inspectors disapprove of its use as a cold-water supply pipe, and therefore it isn't allowed in some regions. Schedule 80 isn't suitable for hot-water supply due to its shrinking and expanding properties. CPVC (chlorinated polyvinyl-chloride) pipe (see Figure 2-2) has the strength of PVC but is heat-resistant, which makes it acceptable in many regions for use on interior supply lines.

✔ **PEX:** The newest type of pipe for residential use is PEX (cross-linked polyethylene). It's approved in many regions of the country. PEX, shown in Figure 2-2, is easy to install because it cuts easily, is flexible enough for gentle bends around corners, and uses compression fittings to join sections together. However, more permanent connections, like from PEX tubing to a copper supply pipe, require a special crimping tool. Another drawback is cost; PEX is three to four times more expensive than copper or plastic.

✔ **Steel:** Many older homes have galvanized steel pipe supply lines and possibly some branch drain lines. Galvanized pipe (see Figure 2-2) is very strong, but it doesn't last more than 50 years. So do the math on the age of your home and your plumbing system to help you determine if your galvanized pipe is worth repair or if you're better off replacing it with copper and plastic. If you do call in a professional to replace it, you should see an immediate increase in water pressure and flow because the insides of galvanized pipes become clogged with minerals over time, resulting in low water pressure.

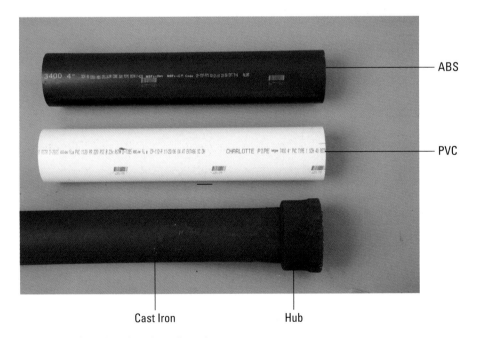

Cast Iron   Hub

ABS

PVC

Figure 2-1: ABS, PVC, and cast iron pipe.

✔ **Copper:** Copper pipe is very long-lasting and resistant to corrosion, which makes it the most commonly used pipe in water supply lines. It's more expensive than plastic but is still a good buy because it lasts and lasts! Copper pipe for residential plumbing use comes in two basic types:

- **Rigid copper** comes in three thicknesses, each with its own letter rating. Type M is the thinnest but is rated strong enough for most residential situations. Types L and K are thicker and used in outdoor and drain applications. All rigid copper, which you can see in Figure 2-2, is cut using a wheel or tube cutter or a hacksaw. Lengths of copper pipe are usually connected with soldered (sweat) fittings. Compression fittings can connect the pipe to shut-off valves.

- **Flexible copper** is often used as a supply line for dishwashers, refrigerator icemakers, and other appliances that need a water supply; you can see it in Figure 2-2. It's easily bent to form even a fairly tight turn, but if it gets kinked, you must cut the piece off and replace it. Sections of flexible copper pipe are joined using either soldered or compression fittings.

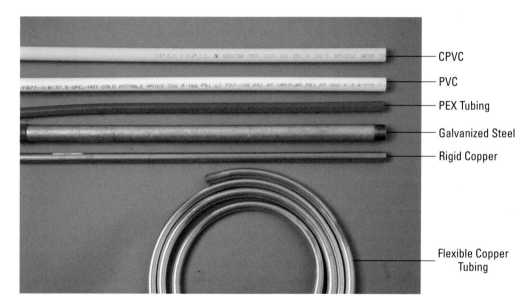

Figure 2-2: CPVC pipe, PVC pipe, PEX tubing, galvanized steel pipe, rigid copper pipe, and flexible copper tubing.

Supply Tubes

To connect a toilet or faucet to a shutoff valve that's connected to a supply line, you can choose from several different types of supply tubes, which are shown in Figure 2-3. They are as follows:

- ✔ **Plastic:** The least expensive option, plastic supply tubes are relatively easy to use. They're easy to cut to length. The downside to plastic is that water flow may be restricted due to the thickness.

- ✔ **Copper:** You usually find copper supply tubes with chrome exteriors for appearance. They need to be cut to length to fit and can't be bent into position because the copper is rigid and will kink or split if bent.

- ✔ **Braided steel:** A braided stainless steel supply tube is a great choice if the tube isn't in plain view. These supply tubes are flexible and even can be looped when in place. The braided steel prevents the inner rubber tube from rupturing over time, a major cause of interior flooding and water damage from dishwashers or clothes washers. Braided steel supply tubes are code-accepted virtually everywhere. They come in various lengths and fitting combinations for faucets, toilets, dishwashers, icemakers, and clothes washers.

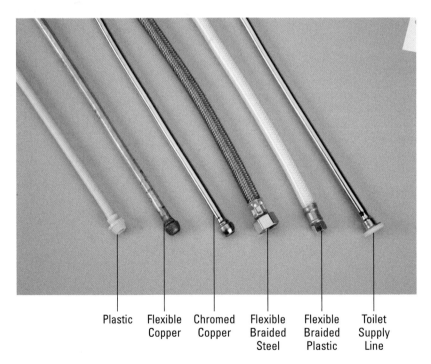

| Plastic | Flexible Copper | Chromed Copper | Flexible Braided Steel | Flexible Braided Plastic | Toilet Supply Line |

Figure 2-3: Plastic, flexible copper, chromed copper, flexible braided steel, flexible braided plastic, and toilet supply tubes.

Supply Fittings

No matter what material you choose for your plumbing supply, most fittings fall into one of four categories:

- **Couplers or unions:** Join pipes in straight lines

- **Elbows:** Turn corners

- **Tees and Ys:** Allow pipes to branch out into new lines

- **Caps or ends:** Seal the ends of pipes during rough-in and final installation

Always buy more fittings than you need; it's my experience that most folks underestimate the correct quantity. Fittings are inexpensive, and buying extra means that you save yourself an extra trip to the store, not to mention a reduction in frustration when you're one elbow short of finishing your project!

Figure 2-4 shows the various types of copper fittings you're likely to use, plus some brass fittings needed to connect copper to fixtures. Keep in mind that copper fittings come in the same sizes (diameters) as rigid copper pipe. Common brass and copper fittings include the following:

- **Brass drop-ear elbow:** You use this fitting in showers to connect the copper supply for the showerhead and/or tub spout. The drop-ear elbow has two wings that you screw tightly to the wall. Drop-ears come in both sweated and threaded styles.

- **Copper supply elbows:** Also called *ells,* these fitting come in 90- and 45-degree angles. A *standard elbow* has two female openings that are the same size. A *street elbow,* which is useful in tight spots, has one female and one male opening. A *reducer elbow* or *coupling* makes the transition between different diameter pipes possible. You also can get reducer elbows that let you change pipe size right after going around a corner.

- **Copper tees:** A *straight tee* has three openings, all with the same diameter. A *reducer tee* has three openings, but one is smaller than the other two; the usual configuration is for the two opposite openings to be the same size with the smaller opening perpendicular to the other two.

- **Copper couplings or unions:** Copper couplings have a center indentation that stops the inserted pipes so that both sides of the connection have the same length of pipe inside the coupling to ensure a solid connection. A *reducer coupler* allows you to join a larger diameter pipe to a smaller one.

Figure 2-4: All kinds of copper and brass fittings.

Drain and Vent Fittings

Plumbing inspectors are sticklers for the correct DWV fittings, so be sure to use the right one for a specific application. Some look almost identical on the outside but are engineered for different applications and aren't interchangeable.

The following list explains each type of fitting to help you get the correct one for your project. Fittings come in various diameters to match the pipe size you're using. As you can see in Figure 2-5, these fittings have hub ends to accept straight lengths of pipe. In order to use these joints, you have to clean them with the proper cleaner and join them with liquid cement adhesive.

- ✓ **Waste or sanitary cross and double-Y:** Both have two branch openings. A reducer connects different size pipes to the waste or double-Y fitting.

- ✓ **Drain elbow:** Also called a *sweep* or *quarter bend,* the drain elbow comes in short, medium, or long radii. Whenever possible, use the long radius bend for better clearing of water and waste. When working in tight quarters, choose from several different size bends: a 60-degree, a 45-degree (or eighth bend), or a 22½-degree (or sixteenth bend).

- ✓ **Closet bend:** This fitting is engineered to accept a toilet flange, which you install after the finished floor surface.

- ✓ **Trap adapter:** Use this fitting on pipe coming out of the wall for a sink drain. You glue the adapter to the drain line in the wall, but its threaded end lets you screw the trap directly to it.

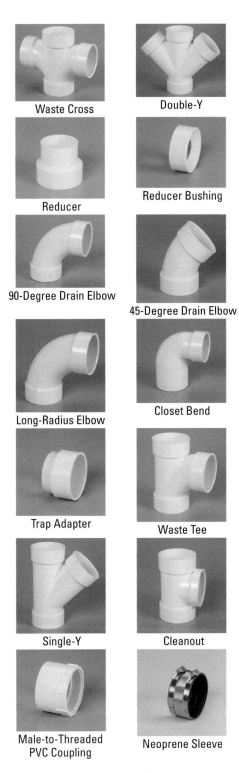

Waste Cross

Double-Y

Reducer

Reducer Bushing

90-Degree Drain Elbow

45-Degree Drain Elbow

Long-Radius Elbow

Closet Bend

Trap Adapter

Waste Tee

Single-Y

Cleanout

Male-to-Threaded
PVC Coupling

Neoprene Sleeve

Figure 2-5: Drain and vent fittings.

✔ **Tees and single-Ys:** These fittings come in all sizes to fit all drain pipes. The two opposite openings, called *run openings,* are in a straight line. The other opening is the *branch opening.* When describing a tee, the run sizes are given first and the branch size is last. For example, a 2½-x-2½-x-2 tee has two 2½ run openings and one 2-inch branch opening.

When buying tees, get waste or sanitary tees, which have a curved, sweeping interior bend instead of an abrupt, hard bend. A sweeping bend has a smoother interior flow design.

✔ **Cleanouts:** Plumbing codes require drain lines to have cleanouts at regular intervals. You either can use a Y with a cleanout or install a cleanout plug to the end of a pipe. Cleanouts are threaded openings.

✔ **Transition fittings:** These fittings are used to connect two different types of pipe or pipes of different diameters. To transition from galvanized steel to plastic drain pipe, use a male-to-threaded PVC coupling. You connect the threaded end to the galvanized pipe and then glue the male end into the PVC pipe. To transition from cast iron to plastic, use a neoprene sleeve fitting. You tighten this reinforced stainless steel sheath around each pipe with screw clamps to form a permanent joint.

Chapter 3

Getting the 411 on Codes and Requirements

Unlike the National Electrical Code (NEC), which applies to electrical work throughout the United States, there's no national plumbing code. Codes vary from state to state and even from city to city, but most are based on the National Uniform Plumbing Code, commonly referred to as the "national code."

Your local code may be much more stringent than the National Uniform Plumbing Code, so check with your local plumbing inspector before, during, and after your project is completed. Your local plumbing code always supercedes the national code.

Most of the repairs I show in this book don't require pre-project inspection or approval; examples include replacing a leaky faucet or installing a new toilet. As the homeowner, you're allowed to make these repairs without an inspection or getting a permit. (Permits are covered later in this chapter.) But a good rule to follow is this: When in doubt, talk to your local plumbing inspector. Inspectors are there to help you through these projects by answering questions and giving advice, but you shouldn't use them as personal plumbing resources or expect them to walk you through every step of a project. Inspectors are very busy out in the field performing inspections and reviewing submitted plans for major remodeling projects and new construction.

For more routine or common plumbing questions, find yourself a good salesperson at your local home center or hardware store. Most have at least one knowledgeable person in the plumbing department whom you can go to for expert advice.

Common Code Requirements

Here are some commonly required code issues that are applicable virtually nation-wide:

 Venting: Plumbing fixtures need venting to work properly. You need to determine whether you need to install a new vent stack or can simply revent the current one.

✓ **Fixture placement:** Fixtures can't be placed too close together. This requirement is more critical in the bathroom, where space is already limited. Here are the minimum space requirements for toilets and tubs: 15 inches between the center of the toilet and the side wall or sink; 1 inch between the toilet tank and the wall; 18 inches between the bathtub and other fixtures.

✓ **Pipe sizes:** The correct size pipes must be used for drains, supplies, and vents. Check your local code for the minimum requirement in your area. Also, find out what type of pipes are accepted in your area for drain lines and water supplies.

✓ **Plastic pipe connections:** PVC is so widely accepted that you're likely to use it for repairing or reworking your existing system. PVC pipe joints must be primed and glued to last. And if you don't prime, the joint will eventually leak! (For more on PVC pipe, flip to Chapter 2.)

Getting Permission — and the Inspector's Blessing!

As I say earlier in this chapter, most of the repairs I show in this book don't require pre-project inspection or approval, and they don't require a permit. In most areas, homeowners are allowed to make "fix-it" repairs to their homes without getting a permit (or as people in the know like to call it, "pulling a permit").

As I state earlier in this chapter, plumbing inspectors are busy people, out in the field inspecting and (hopefully) approving plumbing projects. And if the inspector is inspecting, that means that a plumbing permit was taken out or "pulled" at the local city hall.

The reason for permits is to maintain the safety and uniform quality within your area. If you're not sure whether your project requires a permit, give the city offices a preliminary call or visit. Someone there should be able to tell you what information you need to supply before you start, what inspections are required, and the cost of the permit. The permit fee is usually a percentage based on the total cost of the project.

Chapter 4

Filling Your Plumbing Toolbox

Here's where you can dream and dream and dream about all the "stuff" you think you need to own to be a real do-it-yourself plumber! Fortunately for your bank account, there are some tools (actually, several!) that you really don't need to own for these projects. This chapter covers tools in a way that should help guide you through the sea of options and keep some peace in the family when you ask for permission to buy another tool.

After I discuss the common plumbing tools that are available, I include a very important section on must-have safety equipment for every do-it-yourself plumber.

Tools, Tools, and More Tools

For a small investment, you can assemble a plumbing toolbox that arms you to tackle almost any of the projects in this book. Here are the tools you should own no matter what type of materials your plumbing system consists of.

The following tools are shown in Figure 4-1:

- ✔ **Levels:** A 2-foot level works for checking drain pipe slope on longer sections of pipe. A torpedo level is best for short sections of pipe. See Figure 4-1A.

- ✔ **Screwdrivers:** You should have both a medium slotted and a #2 Phillips screwdriver because plumbing fixtures use both slotted and Phillips screws. A 4-in-1 screwdriver combines both screwdrivers in one tool. See Figure 4-1B-C.

- ✔ **Tape measure:** In order to handle measuring jobs without a helper, get a tape measure that's at least 20 feet long and has a ¾-inch-wide blade. (Narrower blade tapes bend when extended beyond about 8 feet.) See Figure 4-1D.

- ✔ **Files:** You should have both a flat file for general-purpose smoothing and a round (or *rattail*) file for removing burrs from the inside of metal or plastic pipes. See Figure 4-1E-F.

- ✔ **Plastic blade putty knife:** A plastic blade putty knife is recommended to scrape off dried plumber's putty and other hardened debris. The plastic blade is less likely to damage a porcelain surface than a metal blade putty knife. See Figure 4-1G.

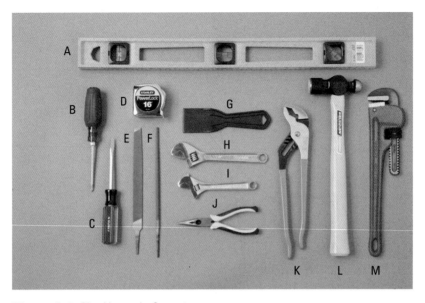

Figure 4-1: Plumbing tools: Group 1.

✔ **Adjustable wrench:** An adjustable wrench is designed to adjust to any size nuts and bolts. Get two sizes: an 8-inch and a 6-inch. See Figure 4-1H-I.

✔ **Needle-nose pliers:** This tool is great for gripping small items even in hard-to-reach areas. See Figure 4-1J.

✔ **Groove-joint pliers:** This tool has several jaw width sizes to accommodate everything from small nuts and bolts to sink basker rings. See Figure 4-1K.

✔ **Hammer:** It's a must-have tool in every toolbox. Period! See Figure 4-1L.

✔ **Pipe wrench:** Use this wrench on all types of threaded pipe connections and fittings. A 14-inch pipe wrench is the best size for most projects. Buy two wrenches if you plan to work on steel pipe because you use both at the same time when tightening some galvanized or threaded copper fittings. See Figure 4-1M.

These tools are shown in Figure 4-2:

✔ **Hacksaw:** This saw, which has replaceable blades, is used for cutting metal and plastic pipe. See Figure 4-2A.

✔ **Socket wrench:** This wrench takes different-sized sockets to handle a variety of nuts and bolts. See Figure 4-2B.

✔ **Caulk gun:** This tool is useful not only for plumbing projects but anytime you need to caulk a seam or joint. The gun pushes a steady, uniform bead of caulk out of the tube as you squeeze the handle. See Figure 4-2C.

✔ **Flashight:** Great for illuminating under-sink areas and other dark places. See Figure 4-2D.

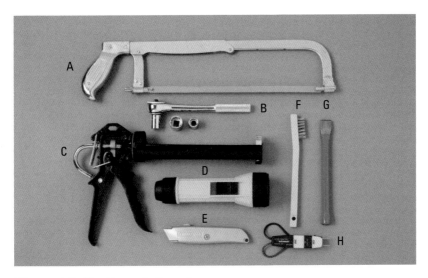

Figure 4-2: Plumbing tools: Group 2.

- ✔ **Utility knife:** This knife is great for cutting a variety of materials. The safest type of utility knife has a retractable blade. The blades are replaceable and can be purchased in multiple-blade packs. See Figure 4-2E.

- ✔ **Wire brush:** A small wire brush is great for cleaning heavily encrusted plumbing parts and pipe threads. An old toothbrush works well on less crusty stuff. See Figure 4-2F.

- ✔ **Cold chisel.** See Figure 4-2G.

- ✔ **Circuit tester:** You use this tool to see if you're getting power to an outlet. See Figure 4-2H.

These tools are shown in Figure 4-3:

- ✔ **Tubing cutters:** To cut copper or plastic pipe, you tighten the screw handle as you rotate the cutter body around the pipe. For most pipe cutting, a standard tubing cutter works fine. A small or mini-tube cutter is useful when working in tight spots. See Figure 4-3A-C.

- ✔ **4-in-1 wire brush:** This brush is a handy tool for preparing copper pipe and fittings for soldering. It has two wire brush ends (one ½ inch in diameter and the other ¾ inch in diameter) and two cleaning holes in the tool body (one for ½-inch copper and one for ¾-inch copper). See Figure 4-3D. If you don't have this 4-in-1 brush, you need to get a reamer brush and a roll of emery cloth.

- ✔ **Flux:** You apply a paste called *flux* to the cleaned end of copper pipe before connecting a fitting and soldering. The flux paste ensures a clean surface for the soldered joint. See Figure 4-3E.

- ✔ **Emery cloth:** Use this cloth to clean copper pipe before soldering. See Figure 4-3F.

- ✔ **Flux brush:** You apply flux with this kind of brush. See Figure 4-3G.

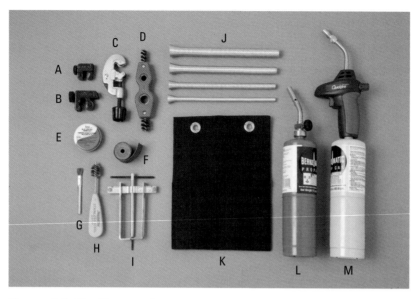

Figure 4-3: Plumbing tools: Group 3.

✔ **Reamer brush:** See Figure 4-3H.

✔ **Handle-puller:** Great for removing stuck fixtures. See Figure 4-3I.

✔ **Tubing benders:** These spring-like tools fit around the appropriate sized flexible copper tubing to gently bend the tubing. Tubing benders usually are sold in three- or four-piece sets. See Figure 4-3J.

✔ **Fiber or safety shield:** When soldering in areas of flammable materials (like wood framing or wallboard), you must have one of these shields to place between the flammable material and the propane tank flame. See Figure 4-3K.

✔ **Propane torch:** This is a generic term for the gas tank setup used for soldering. In Figure 4-3, the torch labeled L requires a spark igniter, and the torch labeled M has an electric igniter. I recommend using MAPP gas instead of propane for soldering because MAPP gas burns hotter than propane, which makes soldering joints with lead-free solder easier. Lead-free solder is required on pipes carrying potable water or water for cooking.

These tools are shown in Figure 4-4:

✔ **Toilet auger:** This auger is specifically designed for clearing toilet clogs when a plunger doesn't do the trick. It fits into the toilet bowl's drain channel and comes with a plastic or rubber sleeve to protect the bowl's porcelain finish. See Figure 4-4A.

✔ **Lock-nut or spud wrench:** This type of wrench is specially designed for removing or tightening large nuts that are 2 to 4 inches in diameter, like a sink basket nut. The wrench's hooks grab the lugs of the nut. See Figure 4-4B.

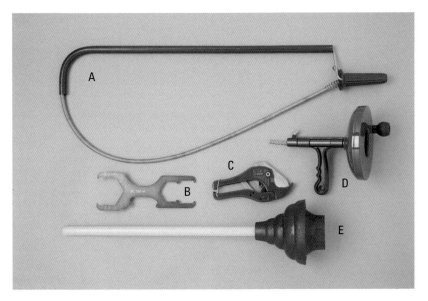

Figure 4-4: Plumbing tools: Group 4.

✔ **Plastic pipe cutter:** A handy tool for cutting, you guessed it, plastic pipe. See Figure 4-4C.

✔ **Hand-crank auger:** Often called a "snake," this tool is a must for every homeowner. It lets you get into drain lines and traps to clear clogs and blockages. See Figure 4-4D.

✔ **Flanged plunger:** This plunger helps you clear clogs in toilets, sinks, and tubs. The funnel-shaped flange fits snugly into the toilet opening to create a good seal for forcing clogs through. To use this plunger on a clogged sink or tub drain, simply fold the flange into the body of the plunger to create a uniform seal over the drain. See Figure 4-4E.

Stocking Up on Safety Equipment — and Using It

Where there's drilling, pounding, or heat, there's the need for safety equipment. And just having it around or in your toolbox doesn't cut it. Safety equipment is there to protect you and your project so don't just have it available — USE IT! Here's a look at what you should have to stay safe in just about every plumbing job (see Figure 4-5).

✔ **Ear protection:** A good set of earmuff-style hearing protectors will preserve your hearing when using noisy power tools. You should also wear hearing protection when you're just hammering; repeated, loud hammer blows eventually can damage your hearing. See Figure 4-5A.

✔ **GFCI-protected extension cord:** A GFCI (ground fault circuit interrupter)-protected extension cord is the best way to protect yourself from shocks (or worse) when using corded power tools. The GFCI shuts off the power to the tool the second (actually the millisecond) it senses moisture. Plug all corded tools into a GFCI-protected extension cord and not directly into an outlet unless you know that the outlet is GFCI-protected as well. See Figure 4-5B.

✔ **Safety goggles:** If your project involves sparks or the chance of flying debris, wear safety goggles. They're also invaluable when clearing drain lines where caustic chemicals may have been used. Styles vary, so choose one that's comfortable but still offers good protection. Even the best safety eyewear is useless if it's so uncomfortable that you don't want to wear it! See Figure 4-5C.

✔ **Gloves:** Both leather gloves and heavy-duty rubber gloves are musts. Leather gloves protect you when drilling, cutting, and soldering, whereas rubber gloves protect your skin when you're clearing clogged drain lines that may contain caustic chemicals. See Figure 4-5D-E.

✔ **Fire extinguisher:** Keep a fire extinguisher nearby and know how to use it if you're soldering copper pipe. A fire extinguisher and fiber or safety shield are the best pieces of protective gear to have when soldering. See Figure 4-5F.

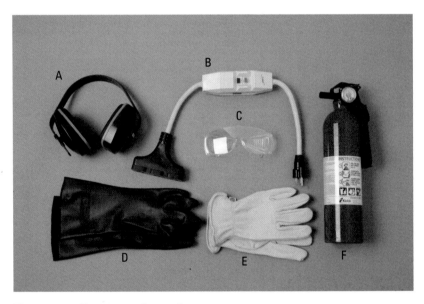

Figure 4-5: Necessary safety equipment.

Part II
Faucets and Sinks

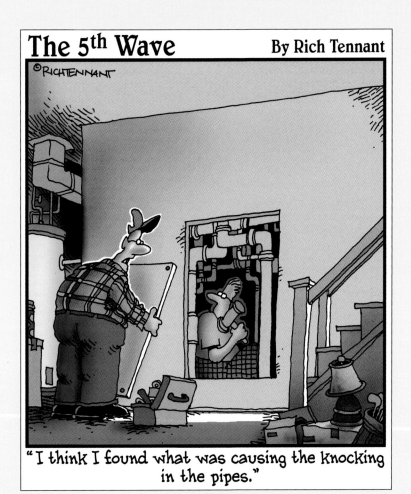

The 5th Wave — By Rich Tennant

"I think I found what was causing the knocking in the pipes."

In this part . . .

This part focuses on two things you surely use everyday: faucets and sinks. And a problem with one or the other (or both!) can really throw a wrench in your day (pun intended). Different types of faucets and sinks abound, but this part focuses on the most common fixtures that you're likely to be dealing with. Specific tasks covered in this part include cleaning faucets and traps to keep water flowing freely, repairing leaky faucets, caulking around sinks, replacing or just adjusting drains, and unclogging drains.

Here are all of the projects in Part II:

- ✔ Cleaning a Faucet Aerator and Sink Sprayer
- ✔ Repairing a Leaky Rotary Ball Faucet
- ✔ Repairing a Leaky Cartridge Filter Faucet
- ✔ Repairing a Leaky Ceramic Disk Faucet
- ✔ Repairing a Leaky Compression Faucet
- ✔ Repairing a Leaky Two-Handle Faucet Spout
- ✔ Caulking around a Sink Bowl
- ✔ Replacing a Leaky Sink Basket
- ✔ Replacing a Sink Trap
- ✔ Replacing a Double-Bowl Kitchen Sink Drain
- ✔ Replacing a Bathroom Sink Drain
- ✔ Adjusting a Pop-Up Drain
- ✔ Unclogging Sink Drains
- ✔ Soldering Copper Pipe

Cleaning a Faucet Aerator and Sink Sprayer

Stuff You Need to Know

Toolbox:
- ✔ Groove-joint pliers
- ✔ Masking tape
- ✔ Paper clip
- ✔ Old toothbrush or small wire brush
- ✔ Small bowl

Materials:
- ✔ White vineger or lime-dissolver solution

Time Needed:
Less than an hour

Hard water is loaded with minerals that build up over time and eventually clog aerators and sink sprayers. So if the water flow from your faucet seems slower than normal, cleaning the aerator and sink sprayer may bring things back to normal. The aerator screws onto the end of the faucet spout and typically has two screens inside that the water flows through. The fix is easy: Simpy unscrew the aerator, disassemble it, clean it, and reinstall. For this type of repair, you usually don't need any new parts. The following steps apply to both faucets and sprayers.

Before you start, place an old towel on the counter next to the sink. This is the best way to keep track of all the parts when you disassemble the aerator.

1. Wrap some masking tape around the jaws of the groove-joint pliers or around the aerator to prevent scratching the surface of the aerator. Grip the outside of the aerator with the pliers, and turn the pliers clockwise to loosen the aerator. You don't need to apply much pressure to the aerator; in fact, too much pressure can crush the aerator housing.

2. Disassemble the aerator by pushing the internal parts out of the aerator housing. A small paper clip might help. If the components are stuck, soak the aerator in white vinegar or lime-dissolver solution (one part vinegar/lime dissolver to one part water) for about 30 minutes or until the deposits are loosened.

3. Clean the parts using an old toothbrush and a gentle touch. Be careful not to bend the screens or you'll have to replace them.

4. Reassemble the aerator parts by inserting the screen, disk, washer, or O-ring (depending on your aerator's design) in reverse order of disassembly.

5. Reinstall the aerator on the faucet by screwing it in by hand in a counterclockwise direction. Use the pliers to tighten securely but there's no need to overtighten. Snug is good!

Cover the sink drain to prevent any small parts from accidentally falling into the drain trap. Also, lay the parts out in the order that you remove them so that you have an easier time putting things back together.

Repairing a Leaky Rotary Ball Faucet

A rotary ball faucet has a smooth plastic or metal ball that rotates inside the socket of the faucet body. Water is dispensed when the handle is moved and the grooves and holes on the ball line up with the seats and springs. If water leaks out below the faucet handle or drips out of the spout, first try tightening the cap or cap-adjusting ring. If that doesn't correct the problem, you need to buy a repair kit and replace the faucet's internal parts, including the O-rings, seats, and springs and possibly the faucet ball. The following figure shows a typical repair kit for this kind of faucet.

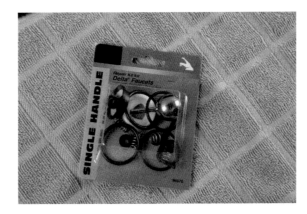

1. Shut off the water under the sink, and turn on the faucet until water stops running.

2. Use a hex wrench to loosen the setscrew in the faucet handle.

3. Lift off the handle and unscrew the cap located under the handle.

4. Remove the plastic cam and cam washer (which usually are one piece) from the faucet body.

5. Lift out the ball. Inspect each part for damage and replace them with parts from the kit as needed.

6. Insert the tip of a screwdriver into the rubber seat in the faucet body, and pull it out. It may take a couple of tries for each seat, so be patient.

7. Insert the tip of the screwdriver into each spring in the faucet body to remove them. You may need to twist the springs back and forth slightly to break them loose.

8. Remove the spout assembly from the faucet to access the O-rings. It can be simply lifted off. Pry off the old O-rings, or cut them off with a utility knife if necessary.

9. Coat the faucet body lightly with silicone grease, and install new O-rings.

10. Install the new springs and seats (in that order) into the holes in the faucet body by pressing them in place with your fingers.

11. Insert the ball in the faucet body so that it sits snugly. The small tab on the ball should fit into the notch in the body; otherwise the faucet won't work.

12. Screw on the cam and cap.

13. Reinstall the handle and tighten the setscrew with a hex wrench.

TIP

If your faucet has a plastic ball, replace it with a metal one. Plastic types can wear out in less than a year, which means that you'll be doing this repair again before you know it.

Repairing a Leaky Cartridge Filter Faucet

Stuff You Need to Know

Toolbox:

- Screwdriver
- Hex wrench
- Groove-joint pliers
- Needle-nose pliers
- Stem puller for your brand of faucet (if you can't remove the old stem with pliers)

Materials:

- Replacement cartridge
- Replacement O-ring
- Silicone grease

Time Needed:
Less than an hour

Cartridge faucets control the flow of water by channeling water through grooves or holes or by way of a tapered cartridge design. Several of the major faucet manufacturers make cartridge faucets and therefore replacement parts, so it's a good idea to take your old parts with you to the store to be sure you get the right brand of replacement parts.

1. Shut off the water under the sink, and turn on the faucet until the water stops running.

2. Remove the retaining screw using a hex wrench or screwdriver depending on the screw. Lift off the handle.

3. Use a screwdriver to remove the retaining nut under the handle.

4. Pull out the retaining clip located just beneath the retaining nut.

5. Unscrew the plastic retaining caps.

6. Unscrew the ring that holds the spout housing the faucet body.

7. Lift the faucet spout straight up off the housing body and set it aside. If needed, clean the faucet body to remove debris. An old toothbrush should do the trick.

8. Use needle-nose pliers to remove the clip at the top of the cartridge.

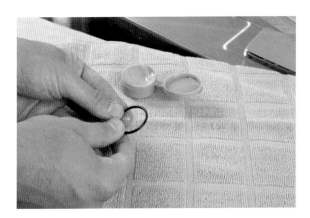

9. With the tip of a screwdriver, slip the old O-ring from its groove and remove it from the housing. Avoid cutting the ring off the housing so that you can take the old, intact O-ring to the store to get an exact replacement.

10. Grip the old cartridge with groove-joint pliers, and pull it straight up to remove it from the faucet body without breaking or damaging either piece. If you can't remove the cartridge using the pliers, you need to buy a tool called a *stem puller*. You must use the stem puller made for your brand of faucet.

11. Clean the faucet body to remove debris.

12. With your fingertip, apply a light coating of silicone grease to the new O-ring, and install it in the groove on the faucet body.

13. Insert a new cartridge or replace the old one if it's in good shape. Reinstall the clip on the cartridge, slide the faucet spout on the housing body, and screw on the retaining ring.

14. Reinstall the plastic nut.

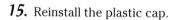

15. Reinstall the plastic cap.

16. Reinstall the retaining nut and clip along with the faucet handle.

17. Turn the water on under the sink, and check the hot and cold water from the faucet to be sure that they aren't reversed. If they're reversed, meaning that turning the faucet to the hot side produces cold water and vice versa, disassemble the faucet, rotate the cartridge 180 degrees, and then reassemble the faucet.

Repairing a Leaky Ceramic Disk Faucet

Stuff You Need to Know

Toolbox:

- Hex wrench
- Screwdriver
- Groove-joint pliers
- Old toothbrush

Materials:

- Replacement cartridge (if needed)

Time Needed:

Less than an hour

Ceramic disk faucets are durable and reliable, but they're subject to sediment buildup that restricts water flow. For that reason, if you live in an area with hard water and find yourself making repairs a couple times each year or more, you may want to consider a different type of faucet. You may be able to fix a ceramic disk faucet by cleaning or replacing the neoprene seals, but most often it's best to simply replace the entire cartridge. This project shows you how to clean the cartridge and replace the seals.

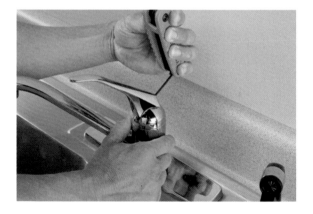

1. Shut off the water under the sink, and turn on the faucet until the water stops running.

2. Use a hex wrench to loosen the setscrew. Remove the handle.

3. Lift off the decorative cap to access the cartridge.

4. Use groove-joint pliers to loosen the cartridge.

5. Lift off the cartridge. You can usually do this by hand. Use groove-joint pliers if the cartridge sticks.

6. Remove the seals on the bottom of the cartridge with a screwdriver.

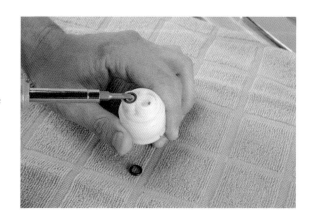

7. Clean the sediment buildup off the seals with an old toothbrush. Also clean out the seal seat area with the toothbrush. If you can't get the sediment and buildup off of the cartridge, replace it.

8. With a screwdriver, remove the O-ring from the inside of the faucet body.

9. Rub silicone grease on the O-ring and seals and reinsert them.

10. Replace the cartridge inside the faucet body and tighten with groove-joint pliers.

11. Replace the decorative cap.

12. Reinstall the handle.

Repairing a Leaky Compression Faucet

Compression or stem faucets have been around for over 100 years and are still in use in a lot of older bathrooms. Their operation is relatively simple: A stem moves up and down when the handle is turned, and a rubber washer at the bottom of the stem pushes against a seat in the faucet body to stop or start water flow. If the washer or seat becomes worn, water drips from the faucet spout.

All purpose or universal washer kits contain various sizes of washers and O-rings. To make sure you get an exact match, take the old faucet stem with you to buy the repair kit. Older faucets may need a packing washer or packing string that usually isn't included in a washer kit but can be found at most hardware stores.

If the stem itself is worn, it should be replaced, but as this type of faucet gets older, parts get harder to find in stores. Replacing the faucet may be your best or only option.

1. Shut off the water under the sink, and open both faucet handles until the water stops running.

2. Use a screwdriver to pry off the decorative cap from the handle (if there is one), remove the screw underneath, and then gently pry off the handle.

If the handle is stuck, gently tap it with the handle of a screwdriver and try to pry it off again. If it still doesn't budge, use a handle puller to avoid cracking or breaking the handle. (Handle pullers are sold at hardware stores and home centers.)

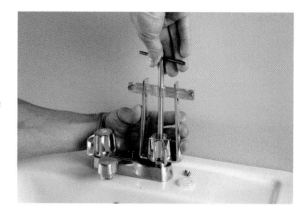

3. Remove the retaining nut using groove-joint pliers.

4. Grab the stem with the pliers, and pull it straight up and out of the faucet housing.

5. If water drips from the spout even when it's off, replace the washer. Remove the screw and install a new washer that's exactly the same size as the old one.

6. If the washer seat, which is located inside the faucet handle body where you pulled the stem from, is worn, replace it. Use a seat wrench to unscrew it — *don't* try to pry it out or you'll damage the faucet body.

7. Reinstall the handle components.

WARNING!

Never reuse an old washer, even if it looks good. New is the best (and only) way to be sure that you won't be doing the same repair again very soon.

Repairing a Leaky Two-Handle Faucet Spout

Stuff You Need to Know

Toolbox:
- ✔ Screwdriver
- ✔ Groove-joint pliers
- ✔ Strap wrench
- ✔ Masking tape

Materials:
- ✔ O-ring kit
- ✔ Silicone grease

Time Needed:
Less than an hour

With a two-handle style faucet, leaks often occur around the base of the faucet spout and from under the spout collar or cap. If you let this type of leak go unattended, it can cause significant damage, much of which you don't see outright; leaking water can get under the faucet's base plate and then drop into the cabinet or into the countertop where it can cause real damage.

1. Cover the jaws of groove-joint pliers with masking tape, and use them to remove the spout cap. (You also can cover the spout cap with tape to protect it.)

If you have one, a strap wrench is a great tool for removing the spout cap because it provides excellent grip and torque without damaging the finish on the cap.

2. Grip the spout near its base and pull up on it. You may need to gently wiggle it back and forth to remove it.

3. Use a screwdriver to pry the O-rings from the groove in the faucet body.

4. With your fingertip, apply a light coating of silicone grease to the new O-rings.

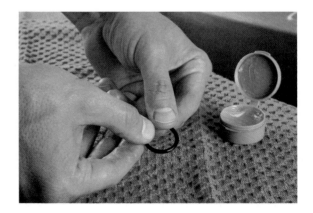

5. Place the O-rings over the faucet body and work them down into the appropriate grooves.

6. Slide the spout back on.

7. Reinstall the spout cap. First tighten it by hand and then use pliers or a strap wrench to complete the job.

Caulking around a Sink Bowl

Stuff You Need to Know

Toolbox:
- ✔ Caulk gun
- ✔ Damp rag

Materials:
- ✔ Tub-and-tile caulk

Time Needed:
Less than an hour

Sealing the joint between a sink and countertop (whether in a kitchen or bathroom) is one task that almost anyone can do. Even better, it's fast, easy, and very inexpensive. Left unsealed, the joint between the sink and countertop allows water to seep under the sink and into the countertop or cabinet, eventually leading to major damage and costly repairs.

1. Cut off the tip of the caulk tube at a slight angle using a utility knife. Tube tips have cutting marks on them which give you different size beads of caulk. Cut off the tip at the first or small dia. bead marking.

2. Insert the tube of caulk into the caulk gun according to the instructions on the caulk.

3. Apply steady pressure to the trigger on the caulk gun to apply a bead of caulk along the joint between the sink and the countertop. Take your time when working along the back edge of the sink and around the faucet.

4. Dampen your finger with water and run it over the caulked bead to smooth it. Wipe your finger on a damp rag periodically to remove excess caulk, and dampen your finger again before you continue smoothing out the caulk bead.

Many people use clear caulk for this job. Don't be surprised when your clear caulk comes out of the tube white. It will dry clear as it cures.

Replacing a Leaky Sink Basket

Stuff You Need to Know

Toolbox:

- Groove-joint pliers
- Basket strainer wrench
- Plastic (*not* metal) putty knife

Materials:

- Plumber's putty
- Drain gasket
- Drain seal (also known as a friction ring)
- Replacement drain basket (if needed)

Time Needed:

Less than half a day

A leaky sink basket can allow water to run down the outside of the drain assembly and drip onto the floor of the cabinet base, eventually causing significant damage. The sink basket assembly connects the sink to the drain line. If water leaks from the basket onto the outside of the drain pipe, you need to replace the plumber's putty seal between the basket and the sink. Doing so requires taking apart the sink basket assembly and the drain line tail piece that it's connected to. In most cases, you don't have to replace the sink basket, just reseal it.

1. Either by hand or using groove-joint pliers, disconnect the slip nut from the underside of the sink basket, and slide the nut down the tail piece out of the way. Move the drain line down away from the basket.

2. Use a basket strainer wrench to loosen and remove the locking nut on the bottom of the basket. (You can try groove-joint pliers first, but most don't open wide enough to go around this type of locking nut.)

3. Scrape off any old plumber's putty on the upper side of the sink with a plastic putty knife. *Don't* use a metal putty knife or you'll damage the sink's finish! If you plan to reuse the old basket, scrape off any old putty under the basket flange.

4. Fashion a rope of plumber's putty that's approximately ¼ inch in diameter. Press it on the underside of the basket flange.

5. Insert the basket into the opening in the sink.

6. On the underside of the drain basket, install a new rubber drain gasket and drain seal, and secure them with the locking nut. Hand-tighten the locking nut.

7. Reconnect the drain line to the basket assembly, and slide the drain slip nut back up into place to secure them. Hand-tighten the slip nut.

8. Test the drain with running water. If you spot leaks, tighten the nut slightly, but no more than one-quarter turn.

Even the best do-it-yourselfers sometimes break plastic fittings, and it's usually that final tightening turn of the wrench that does it. Here's a good rule of thumb: Hand-tighten all fittings and then tighten with pliers only a quarter-turn at a time until the leak stops.

Replacing a Sink Trap

Sink traps, especially ones in bathrooms, usually benefit from periodic cleaning to get rid of buildup and clogs that are too difficult or impossible to remove with a plunger or plumber's snake. The faster and easier way to take care of this problem is to simply replace the trap. Take the old trap with you to the store to get an exact match.

1. Place a bucket under the trap.

2. Loosen the slip nuts with groove-joint pliers, unscrew the nuts by hand, and slide them away from the connections. Be sure to save the two washers that are part of the slip nut connection; you can reuse them with the new trap.

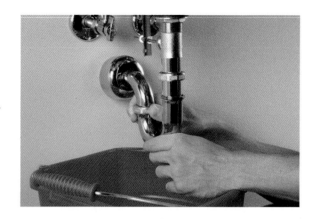

3. Pull off the trap.

4. Slide the two washers from the old trap onto the new trap, and fit the trap into place.

5. Secure the new trap to the drain lines with the slip nuts. Hand-tighten the nuts.

6. Run water in the sink and check for leaks. If you see a leak, tighten the slip nuts one-quarter turn with groove-joint pliers.

If you know or even suspect that chemical drain cleaner has been used to clear the trap, you must take extra precaution when you loosen and remove the trap. Wear rubber gloves and safety glasses to protect your skin and eyes in case of a water splash.

Replacing a Double-Bowl Kitchen Sink Drain

All drains in the U.S. must have a P-trap or S-trap, depending on code requirements. Both designs are engineered to prevent noxious gases from backing up through the drain line into the house. The most commonly found is the P-trap. It's design is quite simple: The bend portion (the "P" section) holds standing water when the drain isn't in use. Each time water is flushed through the drain, the old water is replaced by new water. So why would you need to replace the drain? In a double-bowl kitchen sink drain, over time, food waste and solids can adhere to the trap and eventually clog the trap. The connections also may develop leaks over time due to being bumped, for example, by putting away dishwashing soap and other items under the sink. Sometimes you can simply replace the trap, but most often you're better off replacing the entire drain assembly.

1. Use groove-joint pliers to loosen and remove the old drain assembly.

2. Attach the short tail piece (if needed) to the threads on the bottom of the sink basket. Secure it with the nylon washer first and then the slip nut; slide both up to the basket threads. Then slide on the slip nut and nylon washer that will secure the longer tail piece onto the short tail piece. (Note that this nut and washer go on in the reverse order and orientation of the first ones.)

3. Connect the tail piece, whose length is determined by the position of the drain line coming out of the wall. The tail piece should come to the bottom edge of the wall drain line. You can eyeball this length and cut the tail piece later if it's too long.

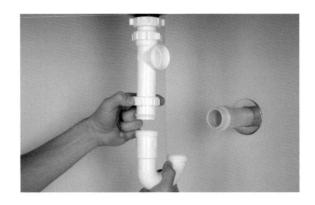

4. Attach the P-trap to the tail piece and tighten.

5. Position the trap arm on the P-trap, and mark where to cut the arm so that it fits in the wall drain line. Remove the arm and cut it to length using a PVC tube cutter or hacksaw.

6. Slide the slip nut and nylon washer onto the cut end of the arm, and inset the arm into the wall drain.

7. Align the arm with the P-trap and tighten; then tighten the arm to the wall drain line.

TIP

Use the old parts as a guide when installing the new parts. Some new pieces may need to be cut, so use the old parts as cutting templates.

8. Attach the short tail piece to the other sink bowl basket with a slip nut and nylon washer. Position the connecting drain line and mark where to cut the drain line so it fits in the opening of the first bowl's tail piece. Then, cut the piece to length using a PVC tube cutter or hacksaw.

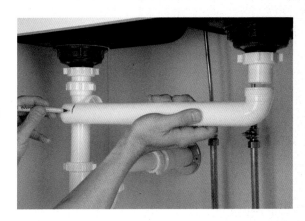

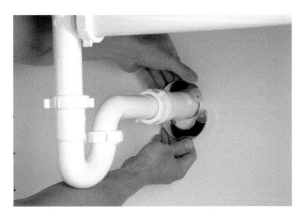

9. Slide the slip nut and nylon washer onto the cut end and insert the cut end into the tail piece. Tighten the slip nut.

10. Secure the other end of the connecting drain line to the short tail piece using a nylon washer and slip nut.

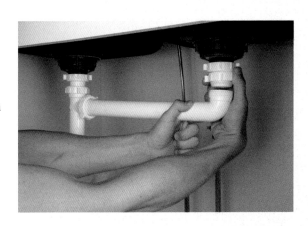

11. Install an escutcheon plate to cover the gap between the wall drain line and the wall. This not only adds a finished look but also seals drafts and keeps out insects. There are two types of plates: A split-ring plate fits around the pipe that's already installed, and a solid-ring plate slips over the pipe before you connect the trap arm to the wall drain line. (In this project, you'd put a solid-ring plate on before Step 7.)

Hand-tightening nylon washers and slip nuts on PVC pipe joints is usually sufficient to establish a secure, leak-free connection. If there's a slight leak, use a groove-joint pliers gently — an eighth- to quarter-turn is usually all that's needed to stop the leak.

Your sink may have a center outlet drain in which a tail piece and connecting arm from each sink basket connect to a center horizontal tee connection, as shown in the following figure. In this setup, you connect the P-trap to the tee in the same manner as you'd connect the P-trap to the tail piece in a single-bowl setup. Then you connect the trap arm to the wall drain line.

Replacing a Bathroom Sink Drain

Bathroom sink drain installation is similar to kitchen sink drain installation with the main difference that a bathroom sink drain uses a drain flange instead of a sink basket to connect the tail piece and subsequent drain line parts. The drain flange on a bathroom sink is still secured from below like a kitchen sink basket, but the securing nut is smaller and can be tightened with groove-joint pliers. A bathroom sink drain kit is likely to have a pop-up stopper assembly that contains the drain plunger used in the sink to stop water flow and a pull-up rod that goes through the faucet and operates the drain plunger. If your existing faucet and drain isn't a pop-up style, you have to replace the entire faucet if you want your new drain to be a pop-up drain.

1. Slide the supplied rubber gasket over the sink drain flange.

2. Craft a snake of plumber's putty that's about the same size in diameter as the width of the drain flange. (It's better to have too much putty than not enough; you can scrape away any excess when everything is tightened.) Press the putty snake around the underside of the drain flange and set aside.

3. Screw the drain body and tail piece together. Hand-tighten the locknut onto the drain threads.

4. Slide the beveled or cone-shaped gasket onto the drain tail piece and thread the lock-nut onto the drain body.

5. Insert the drain body through the sink opening from underneath. Make sure that the drain body is turned so the pop-up connection is facing the rear of the sink.

6. Thread the flange ring from Step 2 onto the drain body from above. Scrape off any excess plumber's putty using a plastic putty knife.

7. Insert the drain plunger lift rod completely through the hole in the top of the faucet. You can adjust the lift height of the rod later.

8. Insert drain stopper into drain.

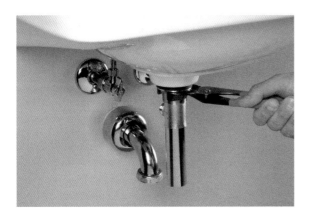

9. Use groove-joint pliers to tighten the locknut until it feels snug.

10. Insert the pivot ball into the opening at the back of the drain body. Secure the pivot ball with the gasket and retaining nut. Don't forget the gasket or the connection will leak!

11. Secure the lift rod extension to the pivot ball rod by sliding the pivot ball rod into one of the holes in the lift rod extension and securing with the retaining clip. You may need to select a different hole if you can't fully open or close the plunger.

12. Test the plunger. The drain should be open when you push down (top photo) and closed when you pull up (bottom photo).

Bathroom drain kits usually use metal-coated parts (chrome or brass are most common) for appearance when the drain is visible, such as with a wall hung or pedestal sink. If the drain is concealed in a vanity cabinet, however, it's perfectly fine to use a PVC bathroom drain kit.

Adjusting a Pop-Up Drain

Stuff You Need to Know

Toolbox:
- Groove-joint pliers

Materials:
- Replacement pivot rod gasket
- Replacement faucet and drain (if old parts are damaged)

Time Needed:
Less than an hour

A pop-up drain has several moving parts that may need adjustments after a while. If the parts seem extremely thin or get bent or damaged, consider buying a new faucet and drain assembly instead of trying to find replacement parts.

Typically, people run into these problems with pop-up drains: The plunger doesn't stay open or closed; water leaks from the pivot ball connection; and either the plunger doesn't lift or it doesn't want to hold water.

If your plunger doesn't stay open or closed: Tighten the pivot ball nut with groove-joint pliers until the plunger stays in either an open or closed position.

Pivot ball nut

If water leaks from the pivot ball connection: Unscrew the pivot ball retaining nut with groove-joint pliers, and remove the rod, ball, and gasket. Replace the gasket, and reassemble the connection.

If the plunger doesn't lift or hold water: Disconnect the pivot ball connection and adjust how it's attached to the lift rod. In this case, you can choose from multiple holes to slide the rod into. You may need a tighter or looser fit, so test the plunger and readjust as needed.

Unclogging Sink Drains

Everyone's household plumber's toolbox should contain an inexpensive hand auger, which can clear most household clogs. It consists of a wound metal cable (or *snake*) with a widened tip that grabs or pushes a clog to clear it. The cable is housed in a plastic case with a handle that allows you to crank the snake when it's in the drain line.

You have the option of renting a power auger, but I recommend that you do so only if you're confident of your do-it-yourself skills. If you rent a power auger, be sure to get complete operating instructions before you leave the rental center.

1. Place a bucket under the sink trap.

2. Dismantle the trap by unscrewing the slip nuts that hold the bend in place.

3. Check to see if the clog is in the trap itself. If so, force the clog out (using an old toothbrush if needed) and reassemble the trap.

4. If the clog isn't in the trap, loosen the auger setscrew and pull out about 12 to 18 inches of cable. Push the cable into the drain line until you feel resistance. The resistance may only be a bend in the drain line and not the obstruction, so tighten the setscrew and crank the auger clockwise until the cable moves forward.

5. Loosen the setscrew, push the cable again until it stops, tighten the setscrew, and crank the auger again.

6. The cable may grab the clog rather than push the obstruction, so if you feel significant resistance, pull the cable out and remove any hair and other junk from the cable.

7. Repeat Steps 5 and 6 until the clog either is removed or is pushed through the drain line.

Wear rubber gloves when working with a hand auger and clogged drain. You'll feel better, especially when you're removing the icky gunk that's clogging your drain.

Soldering Copper Pipe

Stuff You Need to Know

Toolbox:

- ✔ Fire extinguisher
- ✔ Bucket of water
- ✔ 4-in-1 cleaning tool
- ✔ Reamer brush
- ✔ Emery cloth
- ✔ Flux brush
- ✔ Propane (MAPP gas) torch
- ✔ Spark igniter
- ✔ Rag
- ✔ Fiber or safety shield

Materials:

- ✔ Copper pipe
- ✔ Copper fittings
- ✔ Flux (soldering paste)
- ✔ Lead-free solder

Time Needed:
Less than an hour (the number of joints determines total job time)

Believe it or not, soldering copper pipe isn't difficult. That said, it takes practice and patience to make leak-free joints. Why do plumbers use copper? Because it's durable, clean, and can be connected to all other types of pipe and supply lines simply by using the correct transition fittings. Don't get discouraged if your first attempts leak or look a little sloppy. Be patient, take time to practice, and sooner than you think, you'll be soldering with the best of the pros!

1. Be sure all water is drained from the line; water inside the pipe will keep it from getting hot enough to make a leak-free joint.

2. Use the wire brush end of the 4-in-1 tool to clean out the inside of the copper fitting. Tiny pieces of copper (called *burrs*) and grease residue from manufacturing inside the fitting can lead to a leaky joint.

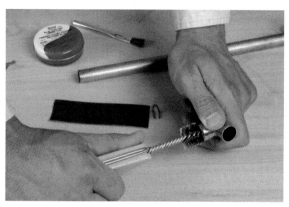

3. Use emery cloth to clean the outside of the copper pipe. Clean the pipe to about the width of the emery cloth. Use a reamer brush to clean the inside of the pipe.

WARNING!

When soldering, keep a fire extinguisher and a bucket of water nearby just in case anything goes wrong! Chances are, you'll do fine.

4. Apply a thin coating of flux (also called *soldering paste*) to the cleaned end of the pipe using a flux brush. The paste should cover about 1 inch of the pipe (the same as the cleaned area from Step 3).

5. Insert the pipe into the fitting and make sure that the pipe is tight against the bottom of the fitting. Twist the fitting back and forth slightly to spread the flux.

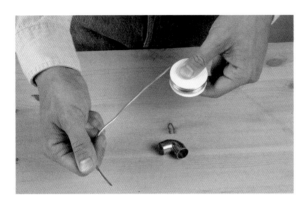

6. Unwind the coil of lead-free solder until you have about 8 to 10 inches extending from the spool. About 2 inches from the end, bend the solder at a 90-degree angle.

7. Light the propane torch with the spark igniter. Hold the tip of the flame about 1 inch away from the middle of the fitting for about five seconds, or until the flux begins to sizzle. Heat the opposite side of the fitting to ensure even heating of the entire fitting.

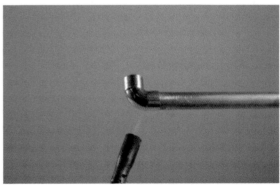

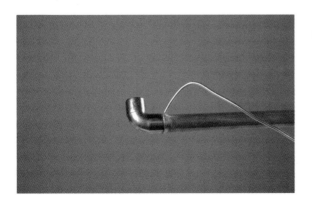

8. Touch the end of the solder wire to the joint created by the pipe and fitting as you continue heating the fitting with the torch. If the solder melts, the pipe is hot enough and ready to solder. If the solder doesn't melt on contact, continue heating the fitting for a few more seconds and then touch the solder to the joint again to check the heat.

Tip: Heat the fitting, not the solder! Heating the fitting allows capillary action to do its thing. Heating the solder will only melt (and waste!) it.

9. Remove the flame from the fitting and quickly insert about ½- to ¾-inches of solder from the 2-inch bent section. An adequately heated fitting draws solder into the joint using capillary action. A properly soldered joint has a thin bead of solder around the entire fitting.

10. Wipe away the excess solder using a rag. The pipe will be hot, so be careful when touching the rag to it!

11. After the pipe and fitting have cooled, turn on the water and check for leaks. If the joint leaks, take the joint apart and resolder it.

Use MAPP gas instead of propane. Fittings need to be hotter to draw in lead-free solder than they used to need to be when leaded solder could be used. MAPP gas burns hotter than propane, thus heating the fittings more quickly and keeping them hotter when the joints are ready to go. MAPP gas is more expensive than propane, but for most home soldering jobs, the time you save using MAPP gas outweighs the extra cost.

Always use a fiber or safety shield (as shown in the following figure) when soldering near wood, especially in floor joists. This flame-proof barrier is available wherever plumbing supplies are sold. It usually has metal grommets so you can hang it from a nail and keep both hands free for soldering.

Part III
Tubs and Showers

The 5th Wave — By Rich Tennant

"You want to look at that new rainfall shower head you installed? It's producing high winds, lightening and thunder."

In this part . . .

Tubs and showers see a lot of action in any home, which means problems with them need swift attention. This part addresses common preventive measures as well as repairs to the parts and pieces of tubs and showers. First you find out how to caulk around these fixtures to keep water where it's supposed to be. Then the part moves on to tasks such as replacing spouts and showerheads and repairing or replacing different kinds of shower faucets. I wrap things up with instructions on adjusting drains to make sure they hold water and unclogging drains to make sure that they don't!

Here are all of the projects in Part III:

- ✔ Caulking the Tub, Tile, and Fixtures
- ✔ Replacing a Tub Spout
- ✔ Replacing a Showerhead
- ✔ Repairing a Tub and Shower Compression Faucet
- ✔ Repairing a Cartridge Shower Faucet
- ✔ Repairing a Disk Shower Faucet
- ✔ Repairing a Cartridge/Seat-Spring Faucet
- ✔ Adjusting a Tub Drain
- ✔ Unclogging Tub and Shower Drains

Caulking the Tub, Tile, and Fixtures

Sealing the joints between a tub, tile, and fixtures is a critical step that many folks overlook. And it's so easy to do! It's important to use caulk engineered for use in high-moisture areas such as the bathroom. Tub-and-tile caulk contains silicone, which makes it long-lasting, flexible, and effective at sealing out moisture under direct water contact. Most people use white caulk, but if you don't want to be left with a bright white line, opt for clear caulk. Just don't be surprised when your clear caulk comes out of the tube white — it turns clear as it dries and cures!

1. Apply caulk to the joint between the edge of the tub and the wall tile. Even though most tubs have a lip along the edges that meet the wall, it's important to seal the joint to prevent water from wicking up behind the tile to the backerboard.

2. Apply a bead of caulk around the joint between the tub spout and tile. Rotate the caulk tube in the gun so that you can apply caulk to the underside of the spout joint.

3. If the bead of caulk isn't smooth enough to your liking, dip your finger in water and gently run your fingertip along the caulk bead to smooth it. Keep a paper towel handy to wipe off any excess caulk from your fingertip as you're smoothing.

It takes practice to squeeze out a smooth bead of caulk from a caulk gun. You may want to practice on a piece of cardboard before working on your tub.

Replacing a Tub Spout

Tub spouts come in two types: those that are screwed onto a threaded supply pipe, and those that are secured to a nonthreaded supply pipe with a setscrew.

Replacing a tub spout is usually an easy project. Just remember to be gentle as you install the new spout.

1. To remove the old tub spout, first look on the underside of the existing spout to see if there's a setscrew. (It's usually in a small slot.) If you see a setscrew, use a hex wrench to loosen it, and then pull to slide the old spout off.

2. Use groove-joint pliers to turn the old spout counterclockwise to unscrew it from the threaded supply pipe. (Don't worry about wrapping the old spout to prevent damage before using the pliers — you're throwing the old spout away.)

3. Clean the threads of the supply pipe using an old toothbrush, and then wrap the pipe threads with two or three turns of pipe-thread (Teflon) tape. Wrap the tape in a clockwise direction to keep it from unwrapping when you attach the new spout.

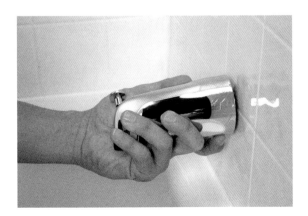

4. Screw the new spout onto the threaded supply pipe by hand until it's snug.

5. Wrap some masking tape around the teeth of your groove-joint pliers and use the pliers to tighten the spout firmly. (The tape protects the pliers from scratching the spout's finish.)

Warning: If the supply pipe is threaded copper, avoid overtightening the spout or you may strip the supply pipe threads.

6. Finish with a bead of caulk between the spout and tile (see the project "Caulking the Tub, Tile, and Fixtures").

Replacing a Showerhead

Replacing a showerhead is usually an easy matter of unscrewing the old one and screwing on a new one. You just have to be careful not to crush or scratch your fixtures with the teeth of your pliers.

1. To remove the old showerhead, wrap a rag around the shower arm to protect it from scratches. Hold the shower arm with pliers and use an adjustable wrench (or pliers) to loosen the showerhead (turning counter-clockwise) from the shower arm.

2. Clean the threads of the shower arm with an old toothbrush and then wrap the pipe threads with two or three turns of pipe-thread (Teflon) tape. Wrap the tape in a clockwise direction to keep it from unwrapping when you attach the new showerhead.

3. Screw the new showerhead on by hand until it's snug.

4. Cover the showerhead and shower arm with rags to protect them, and finish tightening the showerhead using the adjustable wrench and pliers.

Repairing a Tub and Shower Compression Faucet

A tub and shower compression faucet works much like a sink-style compression faucet. The difference is the orientation: The tub and shower version is oriented horizontally (coming out of the shower wall) whereas the sink version is oriented vertically (coming up through the sink). In a tub and shower setup, a two-handle stem faucet has a stem with a washer. The washer presses against the seat in the faucet's valve body to seal off the water flow. If you have a three-handle faucet, the third (middle) handle is a diverter that directs water up to the showerhead or down to the tub spout, depending on the position of the diverter. The most common problem you'll encounter is dripping water from either the hot and cold water handles or the showerhead handle.

1. Before anything else, remember to do the following: 1) Shut off the water! 2) Close the tub drain, and place a cloth in the tub to catch any dropped parts. 3) Buy a washer package that contains the exact replacements you need for your brand of faucet.

2. With the water turned off, open both handles until water stops flowing. Then use a hex wrench to take off the shower handle. If the handle is stuck, don't force it by hand or you may break the handle. Instead, use a handle puller to get it off.

3. Unscrew the retaining clip.

4. Pull off the stem sleeve.

5. If the stem assembly protrudes enough to expose the hex area, loosen the stem with a wrench or groove-joint pliers. If the stem is recessed, use a stem wrench (a deep-socket design made to fit a bathtub stem).

6. Remove the stem.

7. If water is dripping from the spout or show-erhead, replace the worn washer on the back end of the stem. Remove and save the screw that holds the washer, and replace the O-ring with an exact replacement that you've rubbed with silicone grease.

8. Use a screwdriver to pry the O-ring off the middle of the stem.

9. With your fingertip, rub silicone grease on the new O-ring and insert it on the stem.

10. If a new washer doesn't stop the leak, then you need to replace the seat. Use a seat wrench to remove the old seat.

11. Install the new seat.

12. Reinstall the stem.

13. Tighten the stem assembly.

14. Reinstall the sleeve.

15. Tighten the retaining clip.

16. Reinstall the handle and tighten the screw.

In Steps 8 through 10, use an exact replacement washer and O-ring to eliminate leaks.

Repairing a Cartridge Shower Faucet

Stuff You Need to Know

Toolbox:

- Screwdrivers
- Adjustable wrench
- Needle-nose pliers
- Groove-joint pliers
- Hex wrench
- Cartridge-pulling wrench

Materials:

- Repair kit (for your faucet model) or replacement cartridge
- Silicone grease

Time Needed:
About a day

In a tub cartridge faucet, the tub faucet handle only turns the water on and off, and a diverter on the tub spout directs the water to the shower-head or spout. Some cartridge faucet repairs may only require one or two parts, such as an O-ring, but you may find it's just as easy to replace the entire cartridge. Take the old cartridge with you when you shop for a replacement. Many manufacturers have cartridges of varying designs, so having the old one to reference is the best way to get the cartridge you need and save yourself multiple trips to the store. Knowing your brand of faucet is a good idea, too.

1. Before anything else, remember to do the following: 1) Shut off the water! 2) Close the tub drain, and place a cloth in the tub to catch any dropped parts. 3) Identify your brand of faucet. Some cartridges require a special cartridge-pulling wrench made for a specific brand of faucet.

2. Use a slotted screwdriver to pry the cap off of the handle.

3. Use a hex wrench or screwdriver to remove the screw that secures the handle to the cartridge, and remove the handle.

4. Remove the screws holding the escutcheon.

5. Slide the escutcheon off. Behind the escutcheon, you may see a small chrome sleeve or stop tube — unscrew it or pull it out, depending on its design.

6. Use needle-nose pliers to pry out the retaining clip that holds the cartridge in place.

7. Pull the old cartridge out; try pulling it out by hand first, especially if you plan to reuse it (you don't want to damage the stem by pulling it out with pliers).

8. If you can't get the old cartridge out by hand, you may need a cartridge-pulling wrench. Different brands have their own wrenches, which are sold at most hardware stores and home centers.

Tip: Check the orientation of the cartridge before you remove it in Step 7 or 8. It must be reinstalled in the same orientation in order to work properly.

9. If the cartridge looks to be in good shape, replace the O-rings and any other replaceable parts (which varies between brands).

10. Rub the new O-rings with a thin coat of silicone grease before putting them on the cartridge.

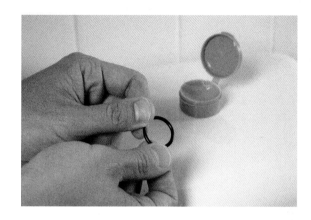

11. Insert the replacement cartridge into the faucet body, making sure it's oriented the same as the one you removed. If your old cartridge isn't in good shape, insert the replacement cartridge.

12. Reinstall the retaining clip.

13. Reinstall the escutcheon.

14. Reinstall the handle.

Repairing a Disk Shower Faucet

Stuff You Need to Know

Toolbox:
- ✔ Hex wrench
- ✔ Screwdrivers
- ✔ Old toothbrush

Materials:
- ✔ Repair kit (for your faucet model)
- ✔ Silicone grease

Time Needed:
Less than half a day

A tub disk faucet works exactly like a sink disk faucet, so repairs are basically the same for both. Don't be confused by the term "disk" and look for a flat, round, disk-shaped part. The disk is actually inside the cylinder; it holds the rubber seals that control water flow.

If water drips out of the spout or around the handle, buy a repair kit for your faucet model and replace all the rubber parts. Inspect the disk for any nicks or cracks, and replace it if you find some. If your faucet has a plastic disk (this is usually the case with less expensive models), replace the entire disk.

1. Before anything else, remember to do the following: 1) Shut off the water! 2) Close the tub drain, and place a cloth in the tub to catch any dropped parts.

2. Use a hex wrench to remove the faucet handle.

3. Loosen the escutcheon plate by unscrewing the three screws (the common configuration on most models).

4. Pull off the escutcheon plate.

5. Remove the ring holding the cylinder in place.

6. Pull the cylinder out of the faucet body.

7. Remove the smaller O-rings from the bottom of the cylinder. Clean the openings with an old toothbrush.

8. If you need to pry the O-ring out using a standard screwdriver, be careful not to nick the plastic housing.

9. Rub a thin coat of silicone grease on the new seats (they should be exact replacements of the old ones) before installing them.

10. Reinstall the cylinder.

11. Replace the ring over the cylinder.

12. Place the escutcheon plate over the cylinder and secure it with the three screws.

13. Reinstall the handle.

TIP

More expensive faucets have ceramic disks that last many, many years. Repairs usually only involve replacing the rubber seats and O-rings.

Repairing a Cartridge/Seat-Spring Faucet

Stuff You Need to Know

Toolbox:
- ✔ Screwdrivers

Materials:
- ✔ O-rings
- ✔ Seats (and other rubber parts)
- ✔ Silicone grease
- ✔ Replacement cylinder (if needed)

Time Needed:
Less than half a day

What may look like a traditional compression-style faucet on the outside, especially by its handle arrangement, may actually be something else. Newer types of three-handle shower faucets use a combination or hybrid type of inner components — generally a cartridge with O-rings and rubber seats and springs. This type of faucet is quite easy to repair when there's a leak, regardless of which handle it's coming from.

1. Turn off the water supply.

2. Pry off the cap of the faucet handle. You may be able to do this by hand, or you may need the help of a slotted screwdriver.

3. Use a screwdriver to remove the screw from the center of the handle, and pull off the handle.

4. Remove the escutcheon plate behind the handle body. It should slide right off.

5. Unscrew the metal cover on the faucet body and slide it off. You should be able to loosen it by hand.

6. Pull off the plastic cartridge extension.

7. Remove the cartridge. It should come out by hand.

8. With a slotted screwdriver, remove the rubber seat.

9. If the spring doesn't come out when you remove the rubber seat in Step 8, remove the spring with your screwdriver.

10. With a screwdriver, pry the O-ring from the cartridge.

11. Use your finger to coat a replacement O-ring with a light coating of silicone grease, and place it on the cartridge.

12. Replace the spring and rubber seat.

13. Use another screwdriver to make sure the parts are pressed in place securely.

14. Reinsert the cartridge.

15. Attach the plastic cartridge extension.

16. Slide the metal cover back onto the faucet body and hand-tighten it. Place the escutcheon plate over the metal faucet body.

17. Slide the handle back on and secure it with its screw. Reattach the decorative cap.

Adjusting a Tub Drain

Stuff You Need to Know

Toolbox:
- Screwdriver
- Rag

Time Needed:
Less than half a day

If your tub won't hold water when the drain is closed, or if the tub drains slowly even after you clear the drain line, then the drain assembly needs adjusting.

There are two types of drain assemblies. Both types use a trip lever, located in the coverplate, to raise and lower the linkage assembly inside of the overflow drain, and both types are adjusted in the same way.

- **Plunger-type drains** have a hollow brass plug (plunger) that slides up and down inside the assembly's overflow drain. When lowered, the plunger stops the water from draining.

- **Pop-up tub drains** have a rocker arm that pivots to open and close the drain stopper.

1. Use a screwdriver to remove the coverplate screws.

 Keep a rag handy to catch any hair or debris on the plunger or pop-up spring.

2. Carefully pull the coverplate, linkage, and plunger from the overflow drain opening.

3. Loosen the locknut on the threaded lift rod.

4. Screw the rod down about ⅛ inch and tighten the locknut.

5. Reinstall the assembly.

6. Tighten the screws on the coverplate. If the drain still won't hold water, repeat the process starting at Step 1.

Unclogging Tub and Shower Drains

A slow draining tub or shower is usually caused by buildup of hair in the drain line. Sometimes you can remove the blockage by snagging it with a piece of stiff wire. And sometimes it can be moved farther into and down the drain using a plunger. But if your drain is still clogged after trying to snag the clog or plunge the drain, it's time to get out the hand auger.

Clearing a tub or shower drain with a plunger:

1. Stuff a wet rag in the overflow drain opening before plunging to prevent air from breaking the suction of the plunger.

2. Place the plunger over the drain to form a seal, and then quickly push and pull the plunger repeatedly until the drain clears.

Clearing a tub drain with an auger through the drain assembly:

1. Lay a rag down in the tub to catch any falling parts, and use a screwdriver to remove the screws of the drain linkage coverplate.

2. Carefully remove the drain linkage assembly from the tub.

3. Push the auger cable into the opening until you feel resistance. Leave about 6 inches of extra cable out of the opening and tighten the auger screw.

4. Turn the auger handle clockwise to move the excess cable into the drain and push the clog down the drain line.

5. Remove the auger and run hot water down the drain. Repeat as needed until the drain runs freely.

6. Reinstall the drain linkage and screw on the coverplate.

Clearing a tub drain with an auger through the tub drain:

1. Remove the strainer cover by unscrewing the retaining screw.

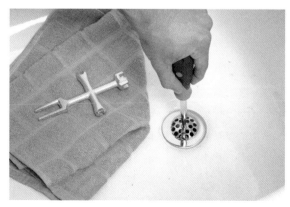

2. Remove the drain basket with a basket wrench.

3. Push the auger cable into the drain. Shower drains have a trap a few inches below the shower floor, so you may feel resistance as you push.

4. Keep pushing the auger cable into the drain until you can't move the cable in any farther. Leave about 6 inches of excess cable coming out of the shower drain.

5. Tighten the auger screw and then turn the auger handle clockwise. Put pressure on the cable as you turn the handle in order to snag or loosen the clog to send it down the drain.

6. Remove the auger and run hot water down the drain. Repeat as needed until the drain runs freely.

7. Reinstall the strainer support and strainer cover.

Part IV
Toilets

In this part . . .

Most people don't like cleaning the toilet, much less working on it when there's a plumbing problem. But it's a fact of life and homeownership that sometimes you have to get down and dirty and address toilet-related problems. This part covers the toilet from tank to bowl (including the seat!). You discover how to check and fix leaks in the bowl or tank, replace the parts hiding inside the tank, and battle the dreaded toilet clog with a plunger or closet auger.

Here are all of the projects in Part IV:

- ✔ Checking a Toilet for Leaks
- ✔ Replacing a Fill Valve
- ✔ Replacing a Flush Valve
- ✔ Replacing a Flapper
- ✔ Adjusting the Tank's Water Level
- ✔ Repairing a Leaky Tank
- ✔ Repairing a Leaky Bowl
- ✔ Stopping a Tank from Sweating
- ✔ Replacing a Toilet Seat
- ✔ Unclogging a Toilet with a Plunger
- ✔ Clearing a Clog with a Closet Auger

Checking a Toilet for Leaks

If you notice water on the floor around the toilet and you know that it didn't come from the kids splashing in the bathroom sink or from the family dog getting a free drink, then it's critical that you find out where the leak is coming from and fix it — now!

Ignoring a leaking toilet does more than waste water. A toilet leak can cause major structural problems both in the floor around the toilet and in the ceiling of the room below. And if your situation gets to that point, you may have to bring in a professional to make some major (and majorly expensive) repairs.

Checking a toilet for leaks is simple and easy. In fact, it's so easy that there are no tools required; you need just a couple teaspoons of food coloring and about an hour to wait and see where the leaks are located. If the leak is from the tank, turn to the project "Repairing a Leaky Tank;" if the leak is from the bowl, turn to the project "Repairing a Leaky Bowl."

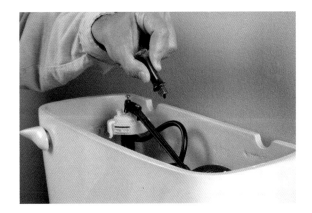

1. Put several drops (8–10 or enough to color the water) of food coloring into the toilet tank. Do the same for the bowl. Wait 1 hour, making sure that the toilet isn't flushed in the meantime.

2. Rub a dry paper towel around the entire base of the bowl where it meets the floor. If you see color on the towel, then the leak is from the bowl.

3. Run another dry paper towel under the tank where it meets the bowl. If you see color on the towel, the leak is from the tank.

TIP

If you find leaks, don't panic. "Repairing a Leaky Tank" and "Repairing a Leaky Bowl" are two projects that come later in this part.

Replacing a Fill Valve

The process of replacing a fill valve is the same no matter what type you have — plunger, diaphragm, or float cup. The fill valve controls the water coming back into the tank after the toilet is flushed. (The outgoing water that goes to the bowl to do the flushing is controlled by the flush valve and flapper assembly; turn to the project "Replacing a Flush Valve" or the project "Replacing a Flapper" as appropriate.)

Toilet fill valves can develop leaks. Hard water causes rubber seals and gaskets to deteriorate, and minerals in the water find their way onto the moving parts of the fill valve, causing them to operate slow or eventually not operate at all. Most folks find that replacing the old fill valve with a similar type is easier than replacing it with a different type because you follow the same steps to install the new valve as you did to remove the old one — just in reverse order.

The most commonly used type of replacement fill valve used today is the Fluidmaster style. It fits virtually every type of conventional toilet tank and has an easily adjusted float cup that regulates the water level in the tank. Updated versions of the more traditional float-arm and ball fill valves have primarily plastic parts now, so they last longer than their old metal counterparts. Either type works fine, so the choice usually comes down to personal preference or the type of valve you're replacing.

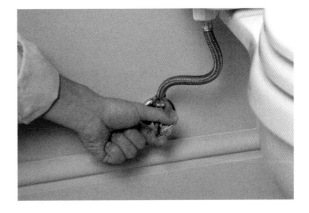

1. Turn off the water supply valve located below the tank. Just turn the handle clockwise to shut off the water.

2. Drain the tank by flushing the toilet, and use a sponge to soak up any excess water in the tank.

3. Disconnect the supply line from the tail piece of the fill valve, located on the underside of the tank. Also disconnect the supply line from the shutoff valve.

4. Drain the tank by flushing the toilet, and use a sponge to soak up any standing water in the tank. Place a bucket under the toilet tank and remove the supply tube, which is connected to the shutoff valve and fill valve.

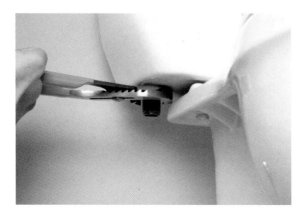

5. Loosen and remove the nut on the bottom of the fill valve; it's located on the bottom of the outside of the tank where you find the water supply feed. Leave the bucket under the fill valve to catch any water that may run out when you loosen the nut.

6. Remove the old fill valve by pulling up on it.

7. Determine the height of the replacement fill valve so that the markings near the valve's top assembly are at least 1 inch above the top of the overflow tube.

8. Twist the bottom of the valve shaft to adjust the height. If your fill valve is different from the one pictured, follow the manufacturer's instructions on how to adjust the valve height.

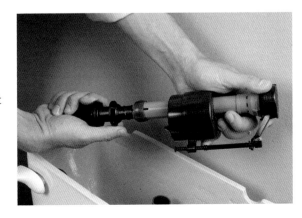

9. Insert the fill valve into the tank, placing the valve's threaded tail piece through the hole in the bottom of the tank.

10. Secure the valve to the bottom of the tank with its plastic locknut. Don't overtighten the locknut; tighten it by hand, and then use your adjustable wrench to go about one-half turn farther.

11. Reconnect the water supply to the threaded tail piece and the shutoff valve.

12. Attach the refill tube and adaptor to the overflow valve.

13. Make sure the refill tube and overflow valve are aligned as shown.

14. Remove the valve top cover or cap. Hold an overturned cup over the uncapped valve, and turn on the water supply to flush the system. Flush the system for about 10 to 15 seconds, and then turn off the water. (You want any debris or rust that may have broken loose when you removed and replaced the valve to be flushed out.)

15. Replace the valve cap by engaging the lugs on the cap and valve body and rotating the cap about one-eighth turn. Ensure that the cap is firmly locked to the valve body or you'll have water spraying everywhere when you open the water supply.

16. Adjust the water level in the tank by turning the screw on the rod next to the fill valve. Some fill valves have a clip that you can slide up and down. The water lever should be about 1 inch below the top of the overflow tube.

Replacing a Flush Valve

The time may come when you need to replace a toilet flush valve and the rubber spud washer that prevents water leaks when the tank water goes into the bowl. Hard water can eat away at the rubber gaskets in these parts and can cause them to fail over time. When that happens, your best bet is to replace the flush valve.

This repair has several steps, but it's one that even a novice can handle if you take your time. The steps will go a little easier if you recruit someone to lend a hand.

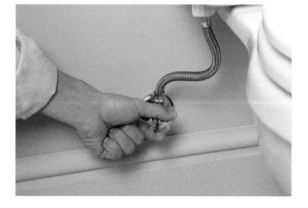

1. Turn off the water supply valve located below the tank. Just turn the handle clockwise to shut off the water.

Take the old spud washer with you when you buy a replacement. Sizes vary slightly and you need the same size or the tank will leak.

2. Drain the tank by flushing the toilet, and use a sponge to soak up any excess water in the tank.

3. Disconnect the supply line from the tail piece of the fill valve, located on the underside of the tank.

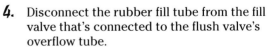

4. Disconnect the rubber fill tube from the fill valve that's connected to the flush valve's overflow tube.

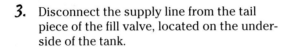

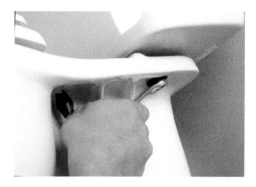

5. Unscrew the tank bolts (one on each side) that connect the tank to the bowl. Use an adjustable wrench to hold the nut located on the bottom of the tank bolt on the underside of the tank (top figure), and loosen the screw with a screwdriver (bottom figure).

6. Lift the tank straight up off of the tail section of the bowl. Turn the tank over onto the towels on the floor.

Tip: A helper makes Step 6 much easier and safer. Toilet tanks are heavier than they look and often require lifting from odd positions if you're working solo.

7. Remove the old spud washer from the threaded tail piece of the flush valve.

8. Use a spud wrench to loosen the spud nut on the bottom of the flush valve. (A spud wrench is specially designed to fit toilet tank spud nuts.) Remove the old flush valve. The flapper is part of the flush valve, so you replace it, too.

9. Install the beveled cone washer onto the tail piece of the new flush valve. The beveled side should face the end of the tail piece. Reinstall the flush valve in the tank.

10. Screw the spud nut onto the tail piece of the flush valve. Hand-tighten the nut.

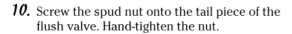
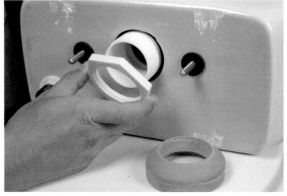

11. Use the spud wrench to tighten it one-eighth turn further.

12. Place the new spud washer over the tail piece.

13. Reinstall the toilet tank with your helper and reconnect all of the parts by reversing Steps 1 through 5.

Replacing a Flapper

Hard water is the leading cause for this repair. Minerals in the water build up on the flapper and around the opening of the base of the flush valve, and the sediment eventually destroys the flapper. The good news is that you can replace a flapper in the time it takes to have a cup of coffee!

1. Turn off the water supply valve. Drain the tank by flushing the toilet, and use a sponge to soak up any excess water in the tank.

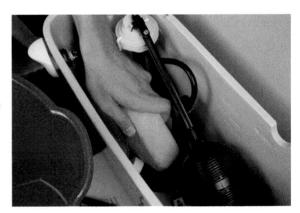

2. Disconnect the chain from the toilet handle flush arm.

3. Remove the old flapper. Most types have slotted tabs that slip over ears on either side of the flush valve (or overflow tube assembly).

4. Line up the new flapper with the flush valve opening, and slip the flapper tabs over the flush valve ears. The new flapper lift point should be aligned with the flush lift arm.

5. Connect the flapper chain to the lift arm.

6. Adjust the chain length as needed so that there's about ½ inch of slack in the chain.

Be careful not to snap off the valve ears when removing the flapper in Step 3. If you break off an ear, you need to replace the flush valve, which I cover in the project "Replacing a Flush Valve."

Adjusting the Tank's Water Level

Stuff You Need to Know

Toolbox:

✔ Screwdriver

Time Needed:

Less than an hour

The sound of running water in an outdoor setting may be serene and relaxing, but slow running water in the toilet means water is being wasted — and you're paying for it! Adjusting the water level in a toilet tank is easy no matter what style of fill valve assembly your toilet has. The four basic types are: plunger-valve ballcock arm, diaphragm ballcock, floatless ballcock, and float cup ballcock.

A little adjustment goes a long way, so make small adjustments and recheck the water level after each adjustment by flushing the toilet and observing the new water level in the tank.

Plunger-valve ballcock arm: Most plunger-valve ballcock arms are brass and are easily adjusted by gently bending the arm up or down. To lower the water level, bend the arm down slightly; to raise the water level, bend the arm upward.

Diaphragm ballcock: The diaphragm ballcock type of valve float arm is usually made of a soft plastic that you can bend up or down depending on whether you need to raise or lower the water level in the tank. Bend it down to lower the water level and up to raise the level.

Floatless ballcocks: These types use a pressure-sensing device to control tank water level. To adjust the water level, turn the adjustment screw one-half turn clockwise to raise the level and one-half turn counterclockwise to lower the level.

Float cup ballcock: If you have a float cup ballcock valve, lower the water level by turning the screw on the rod connected to the fill valve.

Floatless ballcocks are no longer allowed by plumbing codes and really should be replaced with any of the other three types. Turn to the project "Replacing a Flush Valve" for instructions.

Repairing a Leaky Tank

Many times a toilet tank leak can be traced back to the tank bolts that go through the bottom of the tank and connect the tank to the toilet base. Each bolt has a rubber gasket between the bolt head and the tank to stop water from leaking. Another part that could devlop a leak is the spud washer, which seals the gap between the flush valve and bowl. Over time, hard water and minerals cause the gaskets and spud washer to deteriorate and fail. A leaky tank is a common problem that thankfully has an easy fix!

1. Turn off the water supply by turning the shutoff valve clockwise. Drain the tank by flushing the toilet, and use a sponge to soak up any remaining water in the bottom of the tank.

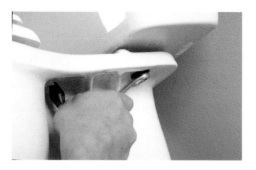

2. Unscrew the tank bolts with an adjustable wrench and screwdriver. You have to use the adjustable wrench to hold the nut located on the underside of the tank bolt, and then use the screwdriver to loosen the tank bolt inside the tank.

3. Remove the tank from the bowl and lay the tank down. (See the "Replacing a Flush Valve" project.) A helper is good to have with this step.

4. Remove the old spud washer.

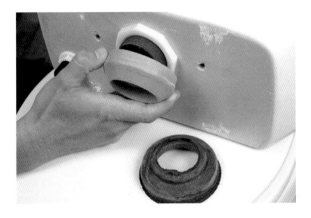

5. Insert the new spud washer.

6. Pull out the tank bolts and gaskets, and use the wire brush to scrape off any of the old bolt gasket that may remain stuck to either the inside or the outside of the tank. You need a clean surface for the new gasket to seat and seal properly.

7. Place the new gasket onto each bolt, and insert each bolt through the holes in the inside bottom of the tank. On the underside of the tank, reinstall the nuts onto the bolts and gently tighten them by hand until they're snug.

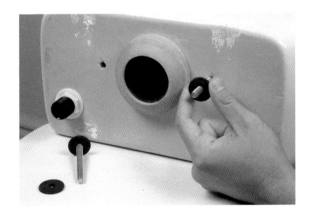

8. Replace the tank on the bowl. Alternating side to side, tighten the bolts and nuts (using the screwdriver and adjustable wrench, as in Step 2) until the gaskets look like they're seated. Then tighten each tank bolt nut another quarter turn.

WARNING!

When reattaching the tank to the bowl, just remember not to overtighten the bolts that secure the tank to the toilet base or you can easily crack the tank.

Repairing a Leaky Bowl

Stuff You Need to Know

Toolbox:

- ✔ Adjustable wrench
- ✔ Putty knife
- ✔ Caulking gun
- ✔ Rag
- ✔ Towels
- ✔ Sponge
- ✔ Rubber gloves

Materials:

- ✔ Replacement wax ring
- ✔ Replacement flange
- ✔ Silicone caulk
- ✔ Plumber's putty

Time Needed:

Less than half a day

Repairing a leaky toilet bowl is one plumbing repair that you need to plan ahead to do because the toilet is out of commission for the entire time of the repair. If it's the only one in the house, you could make a lot of enemies in your family if you don't let them know ahead of time. (Because it's better to be safe than sorry, ask a neighbor if your family can use their bathroom while you make this repair.)

This is a messy repair but one that's made a lot easier if you make room and take your time. Toilet locations usually don't allow for much working room, so remove anything from the toilet area that may get in the way of your work — such as the wastebasket, scale, clothes hamper, and any decorative items. Also, keep in mind that this is a two-part repair: Part one involves removing the tank, and part two involves removing the toilet base (bowl).

1. Turn off the water supply by turning the shutoff valve clockwise. Drain the tank by flushing the toilet, and use a sponge to soak up any excess water in the tank.

2. Remove the toilet tank as instructed in the "Replacing a Flush Valve" project. Set the tank on towels away from your work area so that it's out of your way.

3. Loosen the toilet bowl nuts (which connect the toilet base to the floor) with an adjustable wrench, and remove the nuts.

4. Rock the toilet base back and forth to release the base from the old wax ring, which is under the base between it and the floor drain opening. Get into position so that you can lift the base straight up. If it's too heavy for you, get a helper!

5. Place the bowl on its side on an old towel (to catch any water that may be in the trap). Don't remove the flange bolts unless they're damaged and need to be replaced. If they need replacing, do it now.

6. Stuff a rag into the floor drain opening to prevent gases from entering the house (and to prevent anything from falling down the drain while the toilet is off!). Use a putty knife to scrape off the old wax ring. Also remove the old rubber flange from the drain horn on the bottom of the toilet bowl.

7. Turn the bowl upside down on the towel. Place the new wax ring (with flange) over the drain horn of the toilet.

8. Remove the rag from the drain. Don't forget this step!

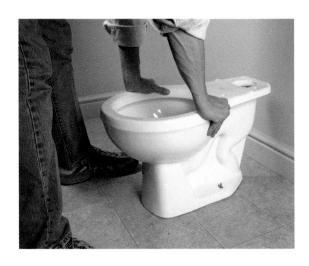

9. Lift the toilet base, and slowly set it down over the flange bolts. Press down evenly on the base to compress the wax ring and properly seat the base.

Use a penny instead of a shim to level the bowl in Step 10. They work great and everyone has some lying around!

10. Level the toilet, using plastic shims (available at home centers and hardware stores) as needed.

11. Reinstall the bowl nuts connecting the base to the floor, and tighten them by hand until snug.

12. Using an adjustable wrench, tighten the bowl nuts gradually, switching from one side to the other to prevent cracking the base and to keep the base level. Don't overtighten the nuts — wrench-snug is tight enough!

13. Put a dab of plumber's putty inside each decorative bolt cap, and put the caps on the bolts.

14. Reinstall the tank as described in the "Replacing a Flush Valve" project.

15. Reconnect the water supply and use the toilet for several days. Check regularly during this time for leaks, and redo this repair if you find that the bowl still leaks.

16. When you're sure that the toilet is leak-free, apply silicone caulk to fill and seal the gap between the toilet base and the floor.

Stopping a Tank from Sweating

Not all toilet leaks come from inside or the underside of a tank. Sometimes Mother Nature and weather conditions play a part in a leaking toilet; humidity can cause condensation to form on the outside of the tank. To prevent this, you need to insulate the tank by lining it with polystyrene foam insulation. All the materials you need are available at home centers and hardware stores.

1. Turn off the water supply by turning the shutoff valve clockwise. Drain the tank by flushing the toilet, and use a sponge to soak up any excess water in the tank. Dry the inside of the tank with an old towel. (The tank needs to be completely dry before you secure the insulation panels.)

2. Hold the foam panel up to the tank and mark how wide the sheet should be to fit within the tank.

3. Cut the foam to the proper width. You may need to angle-cut the bottom corners to fit your tank's contours.

4. Place the foam panel inside the tank and mark the height for the sheet to fit within the tank. Trim as necessary.

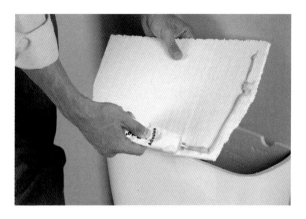

5. Apply waterproof mastic to one side of the panel.

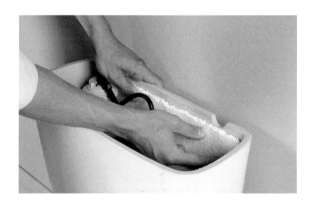

6. Press the panel into place against the corresponding side of the tank.

7. Repeat Steps 2 through 6 for each side of the tank.

8. Let the mastic dry overnight before reconnecting the water supply and flushing the toilet to refill the tank.

Replacing a Toilet Seat

A cosmetic upgrade is the most common reason for installing a new toilet seat. Yes, a seat can get damaged or even crack, but most often the goal is to simply freshen up the look of the toilet. Replacing a toilet seat may be the easiest bathroom repair to make because you don't even need to turn off the water.

Toilet seats come in two basic styles or sizes: round (16 inches from front to back) and oblong or elongated (18 inches from front to back). Measure the old seat before you go shopping or take the old seat with you to ensure that you get the correct size.

1. Pry open the bolt caps with a screwdriver.

2. Use the screwdriver and adjustable wrench to remove the seat bolts, which secure the toilet seat to the base. With the adjustable wrench, hold the nut located on the underside of the seat bolt, and turn the bolt with the screwdriver. After you remove the nuts, lift off the seat.

3. Align the bolt holes of the new seat with the holes of the toilet base. Push the anchor bolts through the holes, and then screw on the nuts from the underside of the bolts until they're hand-tight.

4. Center the seat over the bowl opening and tighten the nuts using an adjustable wrench. Don't overtighten the nuts — just beyond snug is good enough.

Unclogging a Toilet with a Plunger

Stuff You Need to Know

Toolbox:
- Flanged plunger
- Rubber gloves

Time Needed:
Less than an hour

Unfortunately, a clogged toilet is a problem that crops up all too often in homes. Fortunately, clearing a clogged toilet with a plunger is one plumbing project that almost every do-it-yourselfer can handle.

Most toilet clogs are caused by an object that's stuck in the toilet trap and not in the drain line pipe in the floor. Use a plunger to clear blockages caused by waste, both if your toilet is completely blocked and if it flushes sluggishly (in which case, your toilet may be partially blocked). If the plunger doesn't clear the blockage and you're not sure that the clog is from waste, try unclogging the toilet using an auger (see the project "Clearing a Clog with a Closet Auger").

1. Pull on your rubber gloves. Check the water level in the toilet bowl by sticking the plunger into the drain outlet. In order to form a seal around the flange of the plunger, there should be enough water in the bowl for the plunger to be submerged at least halfway. If there's little or no water in the bowl, pour some in.

2. Place the flange of the plunger over the drain outlet and press down to form the seal.

3. Repeatedly press down and lift up on the plunger handle rapidly until the clog clears. You'll know the clog has moved through the drain line when the old standing water goes down the drain. You may hear the rest of the flush too!

Clearing a Clog with a Closet Auger

A closet auger is the tool of choice when an object — like a sponge, a child's toy block, or even car keys! — is the cause of a toilet blockage. A closet auger is designed to grab or snag the object so that you can pull it out of the toilet and not flush it down the drain line as you would using a plunger.

1. Place the auger bend (the covered section that protects the toilet bowl's surface from being scratched) into the drain outlet and push the cable into the trap. Keep pushing until you feel it touch the obstruction.

2. Crank the auger handle clockwise to snag or grab the obstruction. Continue cranking while pulling the auger cable (and the obstruction) out of the toilet.

Part V
The Part of Tens

The 5th Wave
By Rich Tennant

"Why fix a leak with a pipe wrench when a begonia works just as well?"

In this part . . .

In the grand *For Dummies* tradition, the chapters in this part present you with insider tips and recommendations to keep you on track and successful when dealing with home plumbing problems. I start with ten tips for plumbing project success before moving on to ways you can deal with problematic pipes. And because safety is always a concern, I close out the part with ten things to keep in mind as you work to ensure that you remain safe.

Chapter 5

Ten Tips for Plumbing Success

Plumbing repair projects are notorious for sending do-it-yourselfers to hardware stores or home centers more than once over the course of a project, whether it's for tools, extra materials, or a bit of expert advice. Although I can't guarantee that you'll get the job done right on your first try, I can assure you that by following the ten recommendations in this chapter, you greatly improve your chances of plumbing success the first time out.

Try Simple Solutions First

Plumbing problems aren't always as complex and challenging as you may think. In some situations, the simplest solution may be the one that gets the job done. Always start with the simplest fix for the problem, and then logically proceed to the next if the first doesn't work. For example, if the water flow from a faucet is restricted, try cleaning the aerator before you dive into disassembling the faucet.

Work During Store Hours

Whenever possible, plan to work on a plumbing project when you know that stores are open. Don't start a plumbing project at 10 p.m. on Sunday night and expect your local hardware store or home center to be open at midnight when you need that one other part to finish the job. Even if you think you have everything you need for a project, it's best to keep your options open in case a surprise trip to the hardware store is in your future.

Plan, Plan, Plan

Plan out and review the project before you begin. Going through each step helps you identify potential problem areas, saving you time and money.

Know Your Home

Know your home's plumbing system! (I cover residential plumbing systems in Chapter 1.) Before you get started on a plumbing project, identify the location of the main shutoff valve and drain line cleanouts. Familiarizing yourself with these locations and knowing what to do with them allows you to prevent extensive water damage in the event of a major water problem.

Don't Forget the Codes

Investigate and follow your local codes. Plumbing and building codes exist to keep you and your house in safe working order, and it's your responsibility as a homeowner and do-it-yourselfer to be informed. When in doubt, consult your local inspectors to make sure that you understand the codes and are following them properly.

Don't Be a Cheapskate

When it comes to plumbing parts and fixtures, you truly get what you pay for! Buy the best products and materials you can afford. The better the part or fixture, the longer it will last and the more time you'll have between replacement jobs or repairs.

Have the Right Tools

Build a basic tool kit to start. Don't run out and buy every tool we show and explain in Chapter 4; instead, start with the essential tools for making basic plumbing repairs, and add tools as you need them. Don't be afraid to rent tools, too. There's no sense in shelling out hundreds of dollars when you can spend $20 or $30 to rent that tool that you'll only use once in a while.

Ask for Advice

Don't be shy or embarrassed about asking for advice at your hardware store or home center. Most of these types of stores have at least one plumbing expert, so seek out him or her to answer even the most basic plumbing questions. You won't be the first!

Know When to Call a Pro

The first step in solving a problem is accepting that you're in over your head. Then you can take a breath and call in a professional plumber! The longer you wait and the more you try to fix the problem yourself, the more you end up paying the pro to undo your work and then fix things the right way.

Don't Procrastinate

Don't put off minor repairs! A simple repair like a dripping faucet or a running toilet is an easy job — especially when compared to a replacement project that's necessary because you didn't stop the drip.

Chapter 6

Ten Tips for Dealing with Problematic Pipes

I'm sure you've heard people complain about their homes' plumbing pipes banging and rattling or about how a pipe's constantly dripping from a leaky fitting. That's just the tip of the iceberg. Practically everyone's heard a horror story about what happened when a pipe froze and split. Noisy pipes, sweaty pipes, and frozen or leaking pipes are issues that you, the do-it-yourselfer, can actually do something about. This chapter covers ten things you can do to deal with these three pipe problems.

Noisy Pipes

Pipes generally make noise when a water valve is opened, for example when either the cold or hot water valve on your clothes washer is opened. Here are three options you can try to give yourself some peace and quiet:

✔ **Install water hammers.** Water hammers come in screw-on and sweated installation styles, so ask your local plumbing expert which type works best for your situation. For example, the screw-on version is best for noisy pipes leading to your clothes washer, whereas the sweated version of water hammer is best for horizontal water supply pipes that bang.

✔ **Install additional pipe straps or plastic antivibration pipe clamps.** Metal (usually copper) pipe straps are inexpensive and usually do the trick. If the noise or movement is really bad, install a wraparound-style antivibration clamp.

✔ **Wrap pipes with foam insulation.** You can reduce the noise from pipes by wrapping them (both horizontal and vertical sections) with foam insulation. This type of insulation is sold in 3- or 4-foot lengths that are presplit and simply slip over the pipe. Be sure to get the correct diameter pipe wrap; it comes in sizes to fit ½- and ¾-inch diameter copper pipe.

Sweating Pipes

Pipes sweat when a combination of humidity in the air and water running through the pipes causes condensation to form on the outer surface of the pipe. The most common place in the house for sweating pipes is in the basement because of the usually higher humidity there. Running a dehumidifier may help, but there is a better solution.

Pipe wrap (also mentioned in the last bullet of the preceding section) is the best material to keep pipes from sweating. Simply slip it over the pipes, making sure to wrap the corners of the pipes, too, to insure complete coverage and eliminate any chance for condensation to drip.

Frozen or Leaking Pipes

Leaks are never fun, and frozen pipes can fray anyone's nerves. These tips should help:

- **Use plumber's epoxy for a quick fix on a small pipe leak.** Follow the manufacturer's instructions for application to seal the leak — until you can make a permanent repair!

- **Use a piece of $\frac{1}{16}$-inch neoprene rubber and two metal hose clamps to cover the split or leaking area.** Wrap the rubber over the leak, and seal both ends to the pipe with the clamps.

- **Use a sleeve clamp to seal a leaking pipe.** This clamp is hinged and fits over the pipe sort of like a clamshell. It comes with a short length of rubber, which you place over the leak before you put the sleeve in place. Then you secure the clamp over the pipe with the supplied bolts and nuts.

- **Thaw a frozen pipe using a hair dryer or heat lamp.** First, be sure to turn off the water and drain any water that's downstream from the frozen blockage.

- **Wrap an old towel or rag over a frozen pipe at the blockage, and pour hot water over the towel.** Leave the towel in place until the blockage thaws. Repeat as needed by applying more hot water.

- **Protect pipes that regularly freeze by wrapping electric heat tape around the pipe.** Use only UL-approved heat tape, and follow the manufacturer's instructions for installation and operation.

Chapter 7

Ten Safety Considerations

Ⅰf you follow some basic safety rules and use common sense, you can tackle most home plumbing repair projects. Just remember: When in doubt, call in a pro!

Think about Safety Before Anything Else

Keep safety as your top priority. What do I mean? Start by knowing where main shut-off valves are located. Also keep the work area as clear of extra tools and materials as possible.

Don't Get Zapped

If you're making a plumbing repair near an electrical source, turn off the power to that source. Whether it's an outlet or a switch, remember that water and electricity don't mix!

Have Emergency Numbers Handy

Keep a list of emergency numbers nearby. The list should include phone numbers for utilities, fire, police, and medical emergency.

Chill

Take a deep breath, and keep calm! Even if you're facing a burst pipe and water is going everywhere, or if you're dealing with an overflowing toilet, do your best to keep your head and shut off the water source as soon as possible to prevent further water damage.

Practice

Learn how to use a plunger and an auger BEFORE you need them! Your first crack at using such tools shouldn't be under pressure in an emergency situation.

Protect Your Eyes

Wear eye protection. Safety goggles or safety glasses are a must when you're cutting, soldering, or working over your head. Safety glasses provide adequate protection for most jobs, but safety goggles provide the best protection for your eyes.

Protect Your Ears

Wear hearing protection when using power tools, pounding, or hammering. Just because you're "only making one or two cuts with the power saw" doesn't mean that you don't need hearing protection. The same is true when you're hammering or doing some heavy-duty pounding. Continual, loud noise can damage your hearing more than you may think.

Protect Your Hands

Gloves are a must, and even more important, you need to make sure you wear the right type of glove for the job. If you're working where chemicals may have been used, wear heavy-duty rubber gloves. If you're soldering, heavy-duty leather gloves protect your hands from an accidental drip of hot solder. Also, wear long pants and long sleeves to protect you from wastewater that may contain chemicals or carry bacteria. Launder the clothing when you're finished with the job.

Protect Your Lungs

Chemical fumes can be toxic, so wear a respirator when working with or around chemicals.

Use the Right Tools

The first lesson of any do-it-yourself project is to use the right tools for the job. A screwdriver isn't a chisel, and a wrench isn't a hammer! The wrong tool makes the job harder and probably does more damage to whatever it is you're working on. Ultimately, the repair takes longer and costs more money in the long run.

Index

• •

Notes

Notes

Notes

Notes

Want more For Dummies DO-IT-YOURSELF guides?
Check these out

Full-color

DO-IT-YOURSELF
Painting
FOR DUMMIES

Discover how to:
- Tackle a wide variety of household painting projects
- Get the right tools for the job
- Create faux finishes that make your rooms look fantastic!

Katharine Kaye McMillan, PhD
Design consultant and co-author of Home Decorating For Dummies

Patricia Hart McMillan
Interior designer, co-author of Home Decorating For Dummies

978-0-470-17533-0 • $16.99 • December 2007

DO-IT-YOURSELF
Create a Web Site
FOR DUMMIES

Discover how to:
- Create a Web site, from start to finish
- Plan your site, register a domain name, and create pages
- Do it yourself, with step-by-step instructions and illustrations

Janine Warner

978-0-470-16903-2 • $24.99 • January 2008

Full-color

DO-IT-YOURSELF
Plumbing
FOR DUMMIES

Discover how to:
- Tackle a wide variety of household plumbing projects
- Get the right tools for the job
- Save time and money by doing fixes and upgrades yourself!

Donald R. Prestly
Senior Editor, Handy Magazine

978-0-470-17344-2 • $16.99 • December 2007

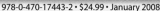

DO-IT-YOURSELF
Web Stores
FOR DUMMIES

Discover how to:
- Set up a Web store from start to finish
- Plan your store, handle sales, and gain clients
- Do it yourself, with step-by-step instructions and illustrations

Joel Elad
Coauthor of Starting an Online Business All-In-One Desk Reference For Dummies

978-0-470-17443-2 • $24.99 • January 2008

DO-IT-YOURSELF
Circuitbuilding
FOR DUMMIES

Discover how to:
- Build electronic circuits, from start to finish
- Create a design, solder, make schematics, and test
- Do it yourself, with step-by-step color illustrations

H. Ward Silver

978-0-470-17342-8 • $24.99 • March 2008

For Dummies DO-IT-YOURSELF guides give you a new way to get the job done on your own. Packed with step-by-step photos, rich illustrations, and screen shots, these value-priced guides provide do-it-yourselfers like you with the how-to savvy you need to tackle and complete common household or technology projects — whether you're replacing a faucet or building a Web site.

FOR DUMMIES
A Branded Imprint of WILEY